THE PURSUIT:

The Chase Of A Lifetime

Ben Jack and Friends

This second edition published 2012 by TVCM & Generation Now, 1 Yarm Road, Stockton On Tees, Cleveland, TS18 3NJ.

First edition published 2010 by TVCM UNIT 211, 70-74 Brunswick Street, Stockton On Tees, Cleveland, TS18 1DW

ISBN 978-0-9565746-1-9

Generation Now
www.generation-now.co.uk

Cover Art by showroomdesign.org.uk

Printed in Great Britain

or all who want to be transformed, because he pursued us first.

CONTENTS

Contents

FOREWORD

I am always having crazy pictures in my head. Recently one of them was of a Ferrari sports car pulling a caravan behind it. The scary thing about the picture is that it's like so many young people that I meet up and down the UK.

The Ferrari is designed for power and speed but is being held back by this huge lumbering caravan. God has designed us to live life to the full – in the fast lane, and yet we drag all kinds of limiting stuff behind us.

I am passionate about seeing young people breaking free from everything that holds them back and living life in the fullness of what God has for them. This is why this book is so important to read as Ben motivates and inspires us to live spiritually in the fast lane, which not only has a huge impact on us but also on all those we interact with throughout our lives.

Mark Ritchie
www.73rdTrust.com

REMIX

INTRODUCTION

I don't know how common it is for an author to get the chance to go back to their published book and rework it, but as an experience, I can highly recommend it to authors everywhere!

The most obvious perk that comes with this process is being able to go and fix some of the problems you notice *after* the book has been printed. These problems are impossible to spot before printing, as they strategically hide, disguised as perfectly well written sentences - the literary equivalent of the classic plastic glasses/nose/moustache combo - only to jump out with a big 'A-HA!' when you get the first printed copy in your hand. Well, in this case, victory is mine. Until I get the first printed copy back, that is.

The thing I am most excited about in producing this remixed version of *The Pursuit* are the additions and enhancements we have been able to make.

The Pursuit

The book is a little longer this time out (sorry for those of you with short attention spans), with additional content in every chapter. There is a brand new chapter all about pursuing after silence which I think is a great addition to the overall theme of the book, and we have three new chasing after sections, covering Authentic Worship, the Image Of God, and the Trinity.

As well as this new content, each chapter has been enhanced with a questions section to help you think a little more deeply about what you've read. These questions can be used as part of a group study, or just for your personal consideration as you try to apply what you have read.

Finally, we have the brand new 'Remix' sections in each chapter. These are short reflections on people or other sources that can inspire us in the areas we are reading about. The 'Remix' section is designed to get you thinking about the theme in a slightly different way, to broaden your understanding of what each aspect of the fruit of the Spirit really looks like. It also revolves around you doing some work; getting online or into another book to find out more. How much you get out of the 'Remix' sections, and for that matter this book, is entirely down to you.

ORIGINAL

INTRODUCTION

If you have picked up this book to read, I can only assume one of two things. Either, you found this copy of 'The Pursuit' left behind on a train and, as boredom has set in thanks to another lengthy delay, your curiosity has gotten the better of you. Or, you have responded to the dare on the sleeve, bought yourself a copy and are now hoping for a transforming encounter with God. Either way, glad to have you on board, although I should warn the reader on the train that the contents of this book are not for the casual-minded. This is a book far more about action than about words.

A few years back, I set out to write a book that, for one reason or another, never came together in the way that I wanted. It was going to be called 'The 11th Commandment' and it started with an epic globe-trotting, Indiana Jones-style hunt for the missing commandment. When our intrepid hero finally finds and digs up the lost stone tablet, the 11th commandment is revealed in all its wonder as,

'Thou Shalt Keep It Real!'

I remember DJ'ing at a Christian festival one year with a group of other guys. To this day I'm not entirely sure why we decided to do this but we set everyone the challenge of signing off every conversation we had during the week with the words 'keep it real'. Maybe it was a throwback to our 80's heritage or something (yeah, I know that makes me sound old) but whatever the reason we all did it, often to comedy effect. Funny thing is, over the years since, it's a motto that has stuck with me. When you think about it, can there be a better encouragement or challenge to us as we look to both grow in our knowledge of God and impact the world for his glory?

When you read the Bible it doesn't take long to realise that that is exactly what God is calling us to. He wants us to be real in our relationship with him and real in our expression of that relationship to the world. It's what we call authentic living.

It's a hard time to be a young person. You

have to face more influence than any generation before you. It's no wonder that so many young people today are struggling with their sense of identity and worth. The media does a great job of convincing the world that so much of this generation is lost, but I refuse to believe that. I'm sick of hearing statistics from inside the church about dropping numbers of youth attendance and what that means for the survival of the church in 50 years. I'm sick of seeing young people being undervalued as simply 'the future'.

You are not just the future; you are also the now! God is calling you to know him deeply, today, and to let that effect a radical transformation in your life. I believe that this generation can be the ones to change the world, not tomorrow, but right now, today! I believe you can live up to the challenge that so many before have failed at, the challenge of true, authentic, Jesus centred living. And the reason why I know you are not simply the future, but the now, is because God has already started the work in you! Dare you now pursue him with all that you are to see that work transform the world? I say 'dare' because this pursuit comes with a cost. It requires sacrifice and it will not always be easy. One thing I do promise you, though, is that if you join in the pursuit you will never be the same again.

> *"But the Holy Spirit produces this kind of*
> *fruit in our lives: love, joy, peace,*
> *patience, kindness, goodness, faithfulness,*
> *gentleness, and self-control."*
> (Galatians 5:22-23)

Over the course of the next two hundred pages or so we are going to look at how the pursuit of God will lead to the fruit of the Spirit being present in your life. Each chapter in 'The Pursuit' unpacks an aspect of the fruit and is supported by a key verse, or verses, which are handily included in the text for those of you who are too lazy to actually look the verses up for yourselves! Joking aside, there is also a 'deeper reading' section for each chapter and this is where I really encourage you to go and do your own reading and studying. The more you put into this book, and this challenge, the more you will get out of it. The same is true of the 'challenge' sections at the end of each chapter. They make for nice reading but even better living.

The prayers that close out each section are an opportunity for you to focus on what you have read and, if you are really serious, to make a commitment before God to the challenges laid out.

I should point out at this stage that I have broken down the aspects of the fruit of the Spirit for the purposes of studying them in such a way that will help us understand them as a whole. We can separate them in this book, but you cannot separate them in your life. When it comes to the fruit of the Spirit, God is all or nothing (actually, that's his call on your life in every area!). Either all of these aspects grow and develop in your life and faith, or none of them do, because they are so interlinked with each other. We cannot pick and choose!

Between every chapter I have invited various guests, all of whom I have huge respect for, to contribute their own thoughts on what this youth generation should chase after. I've been really humbled by what they have all brought to this book, each contributing something close to their heart, in their own style. The breadth of input in these sections, from the fundamentals of faith and the gospel, through to a prayerful desire for purity and even a rallying call for young people to get involved in politics, only goes to show how broad the pursuit of knowing and serving God can be!

The Pursuit

This book is by no means a definitive take on any of the subjects it contains. Indeed, you could write multiple books on each of the subjects we try to broadly look at in each of these chapters. My hope and prayer is that this is the start (or continuation) of a journey that will impact you, and those around you, for eternity.

You've come this far. Will you now dare to join the pursuit?

Ben Jack

1.
the pursuit
of...
LOVE

Key Verse: John 15:9-13

I have loved you even as the Father has loved me. Remain in my love. When you obey my commandments, you remain in my love, just as I obey my Father's commandments and remain in his love. I have told you these things so that you will be filled with my joy. Yes, your joy will overflow! This is my commandment: Love each other in the same way I have loved you. There is no greater love than to lay down one's life for one's friends.

The Pursuit

The first movie that ever made me cry was
Steven Spielberg's masterpiece, 'ET'. I don't
know how old I was when I first saw that film but
to this day I still can't make it to the end without
shedding a little tear. Watching the friendship
between the boy, Elliot, and ET grow over the
course of the film is such a roller coaster ride of
adventure and emotion that, by the time the cute
little alien is >SPOILER ALERT< heading home,
I'm sobbing into my popcorn. The characters
grow to love each other deeply in the film, which
makes their parting at the climax of the movie
incredibly bittersweet. It is, in my opinion, one of
the best films ever made, not least because it
makes the love between two friends, who happen
to be a human and an alien, feel so true.

But, come on, everyone enjoys a good love
story, right? For some it's boy meets girl, boy
loses girl, boy gets girl back in the pouring rain
on the way to the airport type story. For others,
it's the love between two friends or a boy and his
dog. I've seen films where it's love between a
parent and child, a political leader and their
nation, a brotherhood of soldiers, a man and his
sports team. You name it, at some point in film,
television or in a book, every type of love story
known to man has been presented.

Love

For a world that is so obsessed, then, with the idea of love, it's amazing how far wrong we seem to have got it. You see the world is trapped in a cycle of weak, diluted, distorted and perverted imitations of love, whilst the real thing is rejected because of 'the cost'. Let me explain.

Imagine having been without food or drink for days, you suddenly have the purest fruit ever to be grown sitting in front of you. Its very smell is so good it is almost enough to quench your thirst and satisfy your appetite. Before you can consume this fruit, it needs to be peeled to give you access to the goodness inside. Instead of doing that though you pick it up and smash it into the table. From there you hit it as hard as you can a few times with your fists until the juices and mush inside are splattered across the table. You scoop up a little of what remains into a glass but it is not enough to even half fill the glass. Needing the full cup to quench your thirst you decide to spit into the cup but soon run out of saliva. Still not enough. Eventually you have no choice but to top up the glass with a little bit of wee! I know, gross. As disgusting as it sounds, if you were thirsty enough, you would drink it. And yet if you had taken the time to peel the fruit instead of going for the quick option you could have had the perfect drink for your thirst.

The Pursuit

The world is so thirsty for love that it will choose the watered down, spit and urine version of love over the perfect and true love of God because there is a cost attached to it. You see the love of God is both perfect and true (what else in all existence can you say that about?) but before we can have our thirst satisfied we need to realise it does in fact come with a cost. And that cost is me.

"When Christ calls a man, he bids him come and die."

Deeper Reading:

1 John 4:16

1 Cor 13:4-8

John 3:16

Rom 5:8

Gal 5:13

The above quote is from Dietrich Bonhoeffer's classic book *The Cost Of Discipleship*. Bonhoeffer was a German theologian who, during World War Two, was involved with the German resistance movement against Nazism and tragically ended up losing his life in a concentration camp just weeks before its liberation by allied forces. Being a fan of both history and inspirational people of God, Bonhoeffer is definitely a hero of mine. The camp doctor who witnessed Bonhoeffer's execution went on record to say,

> *"I was most deeply moved by the way this loveable man prayed, so devout and so certain that God heard his prayer... In the almost fifty years that I worked as a doctor, I have hardly ever seen a man die so entirely submissive to the will of God."*

Bonhoeffer was a man who knew that to fully accept God's love we must first die to ourselves. When we let go of our old lives and give ourselves completely to new life, in God, we will be forever changed! I love how the doctor notes that at the moment of Bonhoeffer's physical death, he was so transformed by the love of Jesus that he was ready to accept those most awful of circumstances; that horrible execution. Bonhoeffer had died to himself many years before his physical death and because of that he was completely in submission to God's will, whatever the cost!

As inspirational as people like Bonhoeffer are, they can also be a little bit scary for us to look at. I mean, are we really supposed to follow in his footsteps with that level of sacrifice? The simple answer is, yes, but the reality is that, within the world you live in, the stakes are probably not going to be as literally life and death as they were for Bonhoeffer! In your world the consequences may be more about social awkwardness, moving out of your comfort zone, being prepared to stand up for Jesus when it is not the cool or popular thing to do. The question is; are you prepared to give God everything so that you can be transformed by the power of his love?

One thing to remember is that we can never earn God's love. God loves you. He always has and he always will. We do not deserve his love, we are not worthy of it and yet, there is nothing you can do to make God love you more, nor anything you can do that would make him love you less! He loves you perfectly. The point is that for God's love to 'transform' you, you have to accept it fully and be prepared to say goodbye to your old life and enter into new life!

The main thing that distinguishes God's love from any other is that it is perfectly true and therefore unfailing. God will never refuse his love or remove it. When we can reflect that truth as fruit in our own lives, then, we begin to show the world the fruit of love. This is known as the outworking of God's love in our lives. It is literally when we allow the love of God to transform our hearts and our minds to make us more like the real version's of us, that God has always intended for us to be, to make us more like Jesus.

A few years back now, someone used the slogan 'Deliberately Different' to encourage a generation of young Christians. It ended up on wristbands and t-shirts at Christian events and festivals all around the world. Normally I'm not one to go in for the catchy slogan trends but the message behind that one definitely hit the

REMIX:

History and literature are filled with great 'love' stories, from Antony and Cleopatra to Romeo and Juliet. Read up on some of these love stories, and then check out the book 'Crazy Love: Overwhelmed by a Relentless God' (Francis Chan, 2008). What does it mean to love as God loves? How does this compare to the great 'love' stories?

nail on the head in terms of what it means to have Jesus at the centre of your life. We choose to become different to the selfish norm, and embrace the selfless life that comes from loving as God loves. If I were to make a small alteration to the slogan for the purposes of this book though, I would swap out the word deliberately, and instead use 'distinctly' different.

Dis·tinct·ly (adv) clearly or obviously enough to be easily seen, heard, remembered, identified or understood.

To become 'Distinctly Different'; that's what happens when you die to yourself and accept the truth of God's love. We should become 'Distinctly Different' to all that we were, and all that is around us that is not centred in God's love. When we do that, the world will notice and the world will ask.

Summary

- *God's love is perfect, true and unfailing.*

- *The love of God will make us 'distinctly different', transforming us inside out, and we will see the effect on the world around us.*

- *There is a cost: are you willing to be transformed?*

Questions

1. *How would you describe true love?*

2. *What do we learn about God's love from the key and deeper verses?*

3. *Is there anyone that you love so much you would give your life for them?*

4. *What could living Distinctly Differently look like in your world?*

Challenge

Are there things in your life that you have not let go of since accepting God's love? Sometimes we can hold onto aspects of our old lives that keep us from moving forward with God. Write a list of the things in your life that may be barriers to you living a 'distinctly different' life. Give the list to someone you trust and ask them to pray about these things every day. Write a new list every month for a year, and see if you can start removing certain aspects over time.

Prayer

Father God, thank you that you loved us so much that you would send your son Jesus to die for our sins. I want your love to transform my life so that others may see you through me. I want to show your love to the world and be 'distinctly different', so that they might know the truth. Amen.

CHASING

AFTER:

THE WORD

Chip Kendall

In my opinion, the two greatest ways you can transform your life right this very second and in turn model something great for your generation are:

1. Understand that you are 'Jesus with skin on' to the people around you.
2. Completely immerse yourself in God's Word.

Try this. Go stand in front of a mirror, close your eyes and say this simple prayer, "Lord Jesus, thank you for loving me just the way I am. I want to know you and make you known to

27

everyone I meet today. Here I am, send me."
Then open your eyes. The cool thing is that you
will see exactly what Jesus looks like in your
world, staring back at you through that mirror.
You are His hands and feet. You have the mind of
Christ. You are the voice.

Okay, now try this. Make up your mind to do
one thing out of the ordinary today to prove how
serious you are about engaging with God's
Word. Maybe it's reading two whole chapters
before you eat your next meal. Maybe it's
memorising a couple verses by repeating them
ten times in the shower. Maybe it's just leaning
your head out the nearest window and shouting
the first Scripture verse that pops into your head
right now! Be creative. Just do it.

So once you've done those two things, find
me on Facebook and let me know how you got
on.

2.
the pursuit
of... JOY

Key Verse: Romans 5:1-5

Therefore, since we have been made right in God's sight by faith, we have peace with God because of what Jesus Christ our Lord has done for us. Because of our faith, Christ has brought us into this place of undeserved privilege where we now stand, and we confidently and joyfully look forward to sharing God's glory.

We can rejoice, too, when we run into problems and trials, for we know that they help us develop endurance. And endurance develops strength of character, and character strengthens our confident hope of salvation. And this hope will not lead to disappointment. For we know how dearly God loves us, because he has given us the Holy Spirit to fill our hearts with his love.

The Pursuit

Everyone wants to be happy. If you were to carry out a survey amongst any group of people around the world about what they want from life, I am confident the majority would ask to be happy. I know that the 'emo' contingent among us have a certain requirement to look miserable for fashion's sake but, truth be told, no one actually wants to be unhappy!

Happiness is apparently so important that the United States Declaration of Independence has it listed amongst the sovereign rights of man,

"Life, liberty and the pursuit of happiness."

The question is; what exactly is happiness and how do you measure it? One person's happiness could surely be another person's misery. Take a simple example such as sport. If my team wins in a final, that will probably make me very happy. But, what about the supporters of the other team? Can we ever really live in a world where everyone can be happy all of the time? Of course not!

Happiness is temporary. There are times and moments in my life when I experience real happiness but it can't last forever, certainly not in this imperfect world.

When I was 16 my best friend, Dazza, went to Thailand on holiday with his family. When he came back he had brought me a gift, which for a while I thought was the best gift anyone had ever given me; a Rolex watch! I wore my Rolex with pride and made sure wherever I went that people could see my bling! After a few weeks of Rolex bliss I went to check the time one day only to find that the watch had stopped running. No worries, I thought, it must just be the battery. To see if I could encourage it back to life I gave the watch face a couple of gentle taps with my finger and, to my horror, the big hand fell off! To say that I was gutted would be an understatement. As it turns out Dazza, my cheapskate mate, had brought me back a fake watch.

Okay, so I knew all along that it was a fake. But I was still annoyed when it stopped working. I loved that watch and while it was ticking away it was the coolest thing I owned (Which probably tells you a lot about me!). That watch made me

Deeper Reading:

Rom 15:13
1 Pet 1:3-9
Psa 16
Heb 2:12
Jam 1:2-4

really happy for a while but it couldn't last forever. Truth is, not even a real Rolex would have lasted forever. You see everything in this life here on earth is temporary, which may sound slightly depressing, but that is a truth of human life. Go ahead and make a list of things that last forever and see how far you get.

I made a commitment to Christ when I was 10 years old and let me tell you right now that the following years have been full of ups and downs. I've had my fair share of happiness but life has dealt me some heartache too. I am a human being in an imperfect world. For example, I, and those around me are subject to disease and health problems. Christian or not, I've never heard of anyone greeting the news of a life-threatening illness with a dance and a smile.

It's understandable that we would want to pursue happiness and there is nothing fundamentally wrong with that. No one likes feeling down in the dumps and I don't believe for a moment that God wants you to be miserable during your time in this life either! The problems come when happiness becomes the sole pursuit of your life or a more important pursuit than God.

As I travel around and talk to people young and old about faith and God, I often get asked if

REMIX:

George Matheson went blind when he was 20 years old. He wrote the hymn 'O Love That Wilt Not Let Me Go'.
What can you find out about the circumstances in which he wrote that hymn? What does that tell you about how he approached the idea of temporary happiness vs eternal joy?

Christianity is just a crutch for the unhappy. Some kind of self help system that will keep the realities of this depressing world at bay. Perhaps for some people, that is what it is. But that isn't how God views it, and it isn't how he calls us to approach our relationship with him. Is Christianity the cure for sadness? Is God the answer to all unhappiness? Well, yes, but perhaps not in the way you might think.

I once heard a Christian evangelist declare to his audience that becoming a Christian would take away all your troubles and lead to a life of happiness. As a sales pitch that is definitely an enticing idea; give your life to Jesus and be happy for evermore. That's not quite how it works in reality, though, folks. Jesus didn't die so that our lives here on Earth would be all smiles and rainbows! He died so we could have hope for the future; the joy of the eternal life to come.

Take a look at what Jesus says to his disciples in John 16:22, shortly before he is arrested, knowing what was ahead,

> *"So you have sorrow now, but I will see you again; then you will rejoice, and no one can rob you of that joy."*

Because of what Jesus did through the cross and resurrection, no one can take away the joy of the promise of eternal life that he has made possible for us. Furthermore, no one can take away the joy of the Spirit that lives in our hearts when we give our lives to him. That is a very different thing to happiness, which is a temporary emotion. Joy is something spiritual and it is eternal! Check out how Paul backs this up at the beginning of our key verses for this pursuit in Romans 5,

> *"Therefore, since we have been made right in God's sight by faith, we have peace with God because of what Jesus Christ our Lord has done for us. Because of our faith, Christ has brought us into this place of undeserved*

*privilege where we now stand, and we
confidently and joyfully look forward to
sharing God's glory."* (v.1-2)

So, how do we reveal this joy to the world
around us? Well, as Paul suggests in the verses
above, it comes down to faith and the hope that
faith brings. When our faith is bigger than our
emotional state of mind our reactions to life's
situations will be different. You see, no matter
how bad things might get in this life, we have
hope in the future and that has to impact how we
react to what's going on now. It doesn't
necessarily mean that this life becomes easy but
it does mean that, even in the difficult times, we
have hope. However, don't just take my word for
it. After all, I can't put it any better than how
Paul continues in Romans 5,

*"We can rejoice, too, when we run into
problems and trials, for we know that they
help us develop endurance. And endurance
develops strength of character, and character
strengthens our confident hope of salvation.
And this hope will not lead to disappointment.
For we know how dearly God loves us,
because he has given us the Holy Spirit to fill
our hearts with his love."* (v.3-5)

The Pursuit

This is one of my favourite passages in the New Testament. Paul gives us a step by step guide through which we can live lives that are bigger than our temporary emotions. Lives that are grounded in the reality of who Jesus is, and what he has done for us. Lives that have hope for the future. Lives that can reflect something of heaven on Earth today! This is what it looks like:

✻ *Bad stuff happens. Hard times come.*

✻ *We endure the rough stuff and learn through it.*

✻ *We grow in character, we become more like Jesus.*

✻ *We increase our confidence in a perfect heaven.*

✻ *We live to share heaven with others.*

These are the incredible life changing benefits of recognising that your hope and joy rest in Jesus. It all starts with him. This recognition will change your life, and will, in turn, impact those around you who witness this change.

I certainly hope that you know much happiness in your life. But my prayer for you is that, even more so, you will pursue and be changed by the joy of the Spirit in your heart for the rest of eternity.

Summary

- *Happiness is temporary, but joy is eternal (and spiritual), and because of Jesus, nothing and no one can take away our Joy.*

- *We can demonstrate true joy through faith and share our hope with this world.*

- *This joy can offer a glimpse of heaven to those who witness and share in it.*

Questions

1. *How would you describe true joy?*

2. *When the tough times come, how do they affect your relationship with God?*

3. *What does the Bible teach us about Joy? Start by reading the deeper verses.*

4. *What do you think it means to bring heaven to Earth today?*

37

Challenge

You don't have to be a lone ranger in the pursuit of God. Surround yourself with people who are also passionate about pursuing a deeper knowledge of the Almighty God. We live in an age where it is easier than ever to communicate with your friends, so use every method available to drench each other in the joy of the Lord. Our emotions fluctuate, and we have just been looking at the temporary nature of happiness, but the good news is that there is never a bad time to be reminded (and reassured) of the joy we have in Jesus regardless of our short term emotion. So get texting!

Prayer

Lord Jesus, thank you for the cross. Thank you that because of your death and resurrection, I have a hope for the future, and an everlasting joy in my heart. I know that sometimes life is hard, and I ask that your spirit will help me to stay strong in my faith at all times, good and bad. May your joy in my heart impact all that I am, and all those around me. Amen.

CHASING

AFTER: THE CALL

Mike Taylor

"Not that I have already obtained all this, or have already been made perfect, but I press on to take hold of that for which Christ Jesus took hold of me." Philippians 3:12

For what purpose has Christ taken hold of your life? It is for nothing if it is not for the gospel and for the nations! We are saved to be sent! We are set apart for the glorious gospel! We are breathing this very day to take the salvation message to the ends of the earth! So, today I would say that you must pursue that greatest call of God on your life.

"All authority in heaven and earth has been given to me. Therefore go and make disciples of all nations, baptising them in the name of the Father and the Son and the Holy Spirit,

The Pursuit

and teaching them to obey everything I have commanded you. And surely I am with you always, to the very end of the age."
Matthew 28:18-20

"But you will receive power when the Holy Spirit comes on you; and you will be my witnesses in Jerusalem, and in all Judea and Samaria, and to the ends of the earth."
Acts 1:8

Start today, right where you are! Use the gifts and abilities that God has given you to touch the lives of people nearest you. Do what you can today. Then begin to seek and listen to the Lord as he lays on your heart what is next for you. Where he might be leading you to take the Gospel tomorrow. If you are a student sometimes you get lost in the day to day grind of school, studies, homework and you feel like you are not useable now... but this is your Jerusalem, surely he wants to use you here and now! He also wants to use these moments as preparation for all the he has for you tomorrow. So don't miss the opportunity to start today to live the Gospel in your home or neighbourhood or school or anywhere! Be on mission for HIM! Pursue the Gospel today!

3.
the pursuit
of...
PEACE

Key Verse: Romans 8:6

So letting your sinful nature control your mind leads to death.

But letting the Spirit control your mind leads to life and peace.

The Pursuit

I've always been known as a little bit of a dreamer. I wouldn't class myself as someone who permanently has their head in the clouds but I definitely like to let my imagination take hold from time to time. Maybe that's why I have spent an embarrassing amount of thought time working on the acceptance speech for my Grammy award (hey, it's worth being prepared!). Actually, now that I think about it, I have always had a bit of a hopeful dream about winning a significant award for something, I'm not really sure why. Maybe deep down I have some unresolved acceptance and affirmation issues or maybe I just want something for the mantle-piece (yes, I have already picked out the spot).

We all want to be good at something, don't we? Good at our jobs, good at our hobbies, good at friendships, good at school, good at Call of Duty (going online for some multiplayer is usually an embarrassing experience for me as I get repeatedly shot by some ten year old kid in a distant country). Whatever it is in our life that we are active in, it seems we are being rated (often by ourselves) as to how well we do things. If we don't do them to the required standard there is an entire industry devoted to helping us do them better! From self-help books to reality TV shows there's always someone to help with our lust for 'greatness'. Are you struggling with the kids? Get 'Supernanny' in to help and you'll be parents of the year in no time! (I personally object to the title 'Supernanny' as she appears to have no discernible powers. She can't even fly.)

Awards ceremonies are commonplace in the entertainment industry. The film, television and music worlds host a series of international awards shows each year to highlight the best of the best from within their respective industries. I wonder what it must feel like to receive these honours from your professional peers? To be accepted via a little statue into the cream of the crop of your industry? Because that's what it is all about, isn't it; recognition and acceptance? One of the most famous (and ridiculed) Oscar speeches was actress Sally Fields' 1985 effort. On winning her second academy award she took the opportunity to confess,

"I haven't had an orthodox career and I've wanted more than anything to have your respect. The first time I didn't feel it but this time I feel it and I can't deny the fact that you like me, right now, you like me!"

We all feel that need for acceptance and

Deeper Reading:

Eph 6:13-17

2 Cor 13:11

2 Peter 1:2

2 John 1:3

Phil 4:6-7

who on earth doesn't want to be liked? If not by the majority, at least by somebody! The problem is that we often seek acceptance from those who are just as in need of acceptance as we are and sometimes at the expense of who we really are. For many of us the need for acceptance comes down to the need for security in our lives or *confidence*, to put it another way. Ask yourself this; where do you find your security in life from?

I would suggest that the majority of us look to get our security from our family and, to another extent, from our friends and peers. For this to happen we need to be sure that they accept us. In an ideal world it would be great to say that every child is accepted by their parents but tragically, for a multitude of reasons, that is not necessarily the case.

This life can bring with it a good chunk of worry. If you watch the news, every day it seems there is always something new to worry about.

Peace

The world appears to be a pretty unstable place, lacking in much security or peace of mind. And if we can't even necessarily rely on our friends and family to provide us stability, in what other areas do we find ourselves searching for security? Our jobs (or our exam results so we can get the jobs we want), our health, the government, our finances...the list can go on and on. But, you know, just like we were looking at the temporary nature of happiness in the pursuit of joy, so it is with finding security in things this world has to offer. Everything passes with time. Jobs can come and go with the fluctuation of the economy, governments rise and fall and, let's be honest, even the best doctors in the world can't keep you from eventually dying one day.

There is of course someone who accepts us as we are, even in all of our failings and weaknesses. There is someone who can give us security in a world that can offer little or none.

I wonder what God's awards ceremony would be like? Perhaps there would be awards for the most righteous, the kindest, the most loving and the most authentic person of the year. What would you have to do to secure a nomination? Live the life of a saint, presumably. The amazing thing is, God has already held his awards ceremony. There was only one prize. And here is the surprise of the evening; WE ALL WON!

Jesus was our prize and through him we are forever accepted by the love of God. It doesn't matter how good we are at sport or acting or parenting or friendships or Call of Duty (fortunately for me) or anything for that matter. God accepts us, if we accept the prize he has given us - Jesus. A prize, ironically enough, we didn't get for being 'good'. The good news of Jesus brings with it peace, a confidence and security that we have been accepted by him and can move forward through his grace. I say move forward because the Bible actually says that we should wear the peace of God as part of our spiritual armour, on our feet!

"For shoes, put on the peace that comes from the Good News so that you will be fully prepared." (Ephesians 6:5)

The good news of Jesus enables us to go into the world and live this life with confidence and authority. When we clothe ourselves with peace we are prepared for the darkness of this world and whatever unpredictability it may throw at us, we can be confident in Jesus.

Now, just because God loves us and accepts

REMIX:

Most of Jesus' disciples were eventually killed (martyred) for sharing his message. Did you know there are more Christian martyrs today than ever before? What kind of security would you need to have in God to give your life for him? Check out the book 'Jesus Freaks: Martyrs' (DC Talk 2005) and see what you can find out about The Voice Of The Martyrs.

us as we are, no matter what our abilities, that doesn't mean we shouldn't *try* to be good at things! Far from it. We should give our all in life to whatever takes our passion (and some things that don't!). In fact, wherever we do something in the name of God, we should do it with absolute excellence. As Christians we should use the talents he has given us to the max, for his glory. Most importantly we should give our all to living to God's standard for our lives. We should be excellently obedient.

If I was awarded a Grammy for an album I'd produced, I know full well that I would want to make the next record even better, to live

47

up to the title and attention I would get from that award. If I accept the prize of Jesus, how much more so should I live a life that attempts to reflect the significance he brings to my life?

There is nothing wrong with wanting to be liked, or accepted, by your friends, family, peers and colleagues. In fact it is perfectly normal. There is also nothing wrong with wanting to live in a sensible way that gives you an element of security in your life for paying the bills, providing for your family and so on. We do after all live in a world that has certain requirements of us, financial and so forth, to be able to function. However, if any of these things become the focus of your life you will end up chasing your tail, going around in circles, never fully entering into the reality that you can have a spiritual peace and security through having been accepted by the one who matters most and by the one who has your best interests at heart. You have been accepted by the one who has already given you the only prize that will resonate for eternity.

I remember visiting the Reichenbach Waterfalls with my family when I was a kid. This is the famous setting for Sherlock Holmes' final encounter with his nemesis Moriarty. The falls are immense, and after a short journey in a rickety

mountain train you arrive on a viewing platform
where the thunderous sound and raw power of
the falls become fully apparent. It was in this
moment that I began to cry (I am telling you far
too many of my crying stories in this book). I
don't know what happened, but something about
the environment - the power of the falls - freaked
me out and I lost it. I had to go and sit in the
visitors' room until I calmed down My Mum
stayed with me while my Dad and sister ventured
further up into the amazing natural wonder.

When we got back to the base of the falls, I
had calmed down, and was now regretful that I
hadn't managed to go to the top like my Dad and
sister had, feeling that I had missed out on the
experience. It was through no real fault of my
own, of course. Sometimes you find yourself in a
situation that overwhelms you, that fills you with
fear or anxiety. But this isn't how God intends for
us to live. He does not want for us to be held
back by fear or anxiety. He wants us to be secure
in his power, in his will for our lives, and in his
authority over this world.

Sometimes it can be hard to see how God is
in control of this mad world, and indeed there
can be many things in life and in our walk with
Jesus that we struggle to make sense of. The
Bible tells us that God's peace is far greater than

we can fully understand! In other words, the peace that is found in God and can be worked out in your life is too powerful to be fully explained or understood! What this really means is that if we let him take control of our hearts and minds, that very same powerful peace will protect us against even the greatest of struggles, our biggest fears, and will help us to make peace with the things we can't make sense of.

So put your ultimate trust in God, and he will bless you with the spirit of true peace that will give you a different perspective on what it actually means to have confidence and security in this life, because of the good news of Jesus and the prize of eternal life.

Summary

- *Regardless of how good (or bad) you are at anything, God loves you as you are.*

- *Find your security in God, not the things this world has to offer.*

- *The true peace of the Spirit will change your perspective on what it means to have security in life.*

Questions

1. What things do you worry about and why?

2. Where do you find your security in life?

3. How does it make you feel to hear that God loves you as you are?

4. How can we share the peace of God with the world?

Challenge

Read about the armour of God in Ephesians 6:13-17 (see deeper reading). Commit to praying through putting on each item of armour each morning before you leave the house. In particular, when you put on your shoes or trainers each day pray that God's peace will impact your mind and give you confidence to walk as a follower of Jesus in this unpredictable world.

Prayer

Holy Spirit, please move in my heart and in my head, so that I may know your peace. I'm sorry for the times I try to find security only in the things of this world. Thank you, Father God, that you love me as I am, and that I can know true peace because of that. I wholeheartedly accept your prize of Jesus, even though I am not worthy of it. May I use any gifts that you have given me for your glory, and inspire others to do the same. Amen.

CHASING AFTER:

COMMITMENT

Amy Burns

So I have this favourite TV programme. I won't bore you with details but there's this episode in series five when the guy makes a promise to the girl about their relationship. He says to her, "This thing we got going here, you and me...I just want to let you know that I am in. I am all in."

I am all in.
Complete and total commitment.
Wow.

Commitment is not a particularly popular

idea for some people. Most of us like the chance
of a get out clause so we put limitations, or
expectations, on our commitment; "I'll always
love you if..." or "I'll support you as long as..."
Very rarely do we say "I am all in".

And even when we do say it, do we really
live it out?

I once made a promise to God along the
lines of "I am all in". I can remember where I was
when I said it and I know that I completely lived
it out for about ten minutes. But the truth is, it
didn't last. My first year of being a Christian
nothing much changed. I went to youth group on
Friday and church on Sunday but between times I
lived no differently. Apparently, my "I am all in"
was only valid for about five hours a week.

Timeshare holidays were very popular when
I was a kiddie. A number of people club together
to own a property and then each of them has a
particular slot when it's theirs. So, for two weeks
in July every year, that's your holiday home but if
it pours with rain, then tough. It belongs to
someone else in August.

When I became a Christian I had a
timeshare with God. Friday nights and Sundays

were his but the rest of the week belonged to the world.

And I thought that was ok.

I was wrong.

You see God isn't interested in buying a timeshare. He wants to fully invest in you; He wants you all the time. Not because He wants to control you or limit you but because he alone can set you free. From the very beginning this was his plan and his promise of commitment shouts to us from every page of the Bible.

And then, as a sign of complete and utter devotion and commitment to each one of us, Jesus came and lived a blameless life and then died undeservedly. I don't think "I am all in" could be said in any better a way than that. God is committed to us, to me and to you, so surely the question now is, are we committed to him?

After a year or so of living my timeshare life I went back to God and made my promise again.

I am all in.

And I really meant it.

Since then, I have tried to mean it every day of my life, not always successfully, and there have certainly been times when I've wavered and wandered and worldly things have caught my eye. But I've come back. I am all in. As best as I can humanly be.

The last ten years since that moment have been,
extraordinary.
Overwhelming.
Challenging.
Liberating.
And at times very, very hard.

But the thing is, I would never go back to my timeshare with God. It's just a bit tacky. There is so much more on offer for me and for you, if we can come wholeheartedly and say "I am all in". Let's really go for it. Let's be committed and devoted, fully given over to His plan for us, trusting in his promises. Let's grab a hold of God's hand and see where he takes us. Let's chase after complete commitment.

4.
the pursuit of...
PATIENCE

Key Verse: Romans 12:12

Rejoice in our confident hope.

Be patient in trouble,

and keep on praying.

The Pursuit

A few years ago, I was asked to star in a movie. Okay, maybe 'star' is slightly misleading. I was asked to appear in a movie, very briefly. The producers and I had a conversation about featuring some music in the film that I had released as part of a DJ group called Aorta, and as part of the deal they wanted us to make a little cameo appearance in a wedding scene as - yep you guessed it - the wedding DJ's. I know, really stretching our acting muscles.

We wrapped the first scene pretty quickly and did a great job of looking like genuine wedding DJ's! The director then asked us if we could stick around to feature in a flashback scene, also set at a wedding. Fine, we thought, it was easy enough the first time. For this scene, though, we would have to get changed into a different costume. Now, anyone who knows me will know that I'm a hat person. It's very rare that you will see me out and about without some form of headwear on. It's like my trademark; pirates have parrots and I have hats. The problem was, the production didn't have another hat for me to wear, which meant that I was going to have to go on screen...without a hat! The director convinced me that the hair and makeup department would make me look fabulous so I had nothing to worry about. These people are professionals, I thought, so I decided to put my trust in them.

After 10 minutes with the 'make Ben's hair cool lady' (I don't think that was her official title), she was finished and offered me a mirror so I could see just how I was going to be immortalised on film. I held the mirror in front of my face and, apparently, it took them five minutes to stop me screaming. I can't remember; I must have passed out. For a reason I will never understand, hair lady had decided to give me the kind of slicked-down comb-over that was probably last in fashion around 1926. Quite frankly, it made me look like a Lego man who's head had been melted. It was the worst hairstyle I had ever had. Ever. And now, it was going to be captured on film for the world to see. Thanks very much, hair lady. So much for trusting the professionals.

We all have to put our trust in various things and various people through our lives. Every day that I get into my car I put my trust in the brakes working so that I stop when I want to, instead of stopping in the car in front. Some things we put our trust in are more significant, like the doctors who treat a serious illness. Others are more trivial in the grand scheme of things, but can still

**Deeper
Reading:**

Eccl 7:8-9

Psa 37:7

Psa 40:1

Rom 15:5

Col 1:11

Titus 2:2

carry significance for the people involved; like the keeping of a little secret between friends.

One thing I'm sure we can all agree on is that no one likes to have their trust broken. And yet I'm sure, at some point, we have all been let down by somebody we trusted, in some way.

Have you ever bought or sold something on eBay? I love to search out a bargain on the Internet and eBay is usually a good place to find someone selling something they don't want, but that you really do! The only problem with eBay is that you never actually know who you are buying from. There is a certain amount of seller information and a feedback history to help guide you, but, ultimately, you have to trust that once you have paid your money the seller is honest enough to send you your treasure. I remember trying to buy some James Bond-related merchandise one time, only for it to never turn up at my house, even after I had paid. When I chased it up with the post office a few weeks later they sent me a proof of delivery slip apparently showing they had delivered it and that I had signed for the item. The address was correct but guess what the signature on the slip was... J. Bond! Sometimes it seems like you can't trust anyone.

The people I value most in my life are the ones I feel I can put my trust in the most. I know that, to the best of their ability, my family and my best friends would never intentionally let me down. It's really important to have people in your life that you can rely on. But at the same time it would be foolish of us to expect them to be perfect all the time. We are all human; we all get it wrong at times. Can you guess where I'm going with this?

You can put your complete trust in God. He will never let you down. It really is quite an amazing concept to think that the God of all creation, the entire universe, is interested in you as an individual and he wants you to put your trust in him so that he can work in your life.

Trusting God is the first step to living a patient life. We all have moments when we get impatient, don't we? Some people have higher tolerance levels than others but even the most patient people have a breaking point! My parents used to make me wait on Christmas day to open my presents until all the family was around in the afternoon. I can remember the absolute agony, as a child, of being able to see the presents that Santa had delivered sitting under the tree but not actually being allowed to rip the paper off and see what was inside. Shame on you, Mum and Dad, for inflicting such trauma on me as a child! Actually, often the waiting would build such an excitement in me that by the time it was the moment to open up the presents it was an even sweeter experience. I certainly have so many happy memories of those times and yet, in many cases, could not actually tell you what the specific presents were.

Still, it is true that sometimes having a patient attitude towards things can be very difficult, especially for an impulsive person like me! During times of uncertainty, or even suffering, our patience can be the first thing to go out of the window. But what does that say about our trust in God? Complete trust in the almighty God and complete submission to his will, will transform our hearts into patient (and peaceful) hearts and when we demonstrate our willingness to be patient, we demonstrate real faithfulness!

Patience

Worry, anxiety, distrust, fear, annoyance and anger, these are all things that are completely counter to patience. Can you see how damaging those things can be in life? God's Word consistently speaks against such things:

Worry	*Luke 12:22-26*
Anxiety	*Philippians 4:6-7*
Distrust	Proverbs 3:5
Fear	*Hebrews 13:6*
Annoyance	Proverbs 12:16
Anger	*James 1:19-20*

How many of the world's problems can you file under one of those headings? We live in such alarming times brought about by a world so lacking in trust and patience. But God has a better plan, a plan to move us away from the negative things and replace them with a willingness to hold firm to him, to his work and purpose for us. If we can give our all to eradicating such things as distrust and fear through patient lives, there is no question that we will impact the world around us and stand apart for the glory of God, the one in whom the world so desperately needs to place their trust.

"Dear brothers and sisters, when troubles come your way, consider it an opportunity for great joy. For you know that when your faith is tested, your endurance has a chance to grow. So let it grow, for when your endurance is fully developed, you will be perfect and complete, needing nothing." (James 1:2-4)

I'm always amazed by endurance athletes, who run ridiculously long distances, which would probably kill any normal individual! I'm probably so impressed because I have no athletic stamina whatsoever. Case in point, and also another example of how my Dad used to torment me as a kid (you didn't think I'd stay silent forever, did you Dad?), was by dragging me up and down mountains on holiday, promising that the view would be worth it when we got to the top! My little legs used to ache as we would trudge about the mountainsides (I'd like you to picture Everest levels of climbing at this point, although there is some artistic license involved). But as much as I hate to admit it, the old fella was right; it was always worth enduring the struggle for the view.

I know for many of you reading this, the things you have had to and are having to endure are far more significant and difficult than going on a long walk, but the truth remains - patience helps us to endure even the hardest sufferings, and keep our eyes fixed on God.

True patience often takes time to acquire. We have to be patient as we work towards becoming patient! If you start demanding that God make you patient now, it doesn't really work, does it? Trust in God, match

> **REMIX:**
> *Our understanding of God is key to placing our full trust in him. Studying His Word helps us to know Him more fully, but can be challenging and requires patience. 'How To Read The Bible For All It's Worth' (Fee/Stuart. Third Ed.2003) will help you to read the Bible in a full and understandable way.*

your heart with his and give him the time he requires to create a new work in you. Your patience, like a child on Christmas day, will be rewarded. Your endurance, like a walk up the mountain, will be worth the view.

Summary

- *Put your complete trust in God, he will never let you down.*

- *Worry, distrust, fear, annoyance and anger can all be overcome through patience and trust in God.*

- *Life is an endurance race, not a sprint. Patience will help you endure through even the hardest sufferings.*

Questions

1. *How patient do you think you are?*

2. *What are the things in life that cause you to lose patience?*

3. *If trusting God is the key to patience, how can we learn to trust God more?*

4. *What impact will the fruit of patience lived out have in the world around you?*

Challenge

Buy yourself a notebook and keep it somewhere handy. At least once a week take the time to write down all the good things and all the bad things that have been going on in your life. Set some time aside during this process to patiently listen to God and if you feel you have heard something from him, jot that down too. After a few months you will have what I like to call an 'Endurance Journal'. The highs and lows of your life laid out before you can really put things into perspective, in both the good, and bad times. What has God been saying to you in those times?

Prayer

Father God, help me to put my complete trust in you. Thank you that you will never let me down. Help me to effect change in the world by setting an example of patience and revealing you as the hope for the world to trust in. I pray that in the hardest times of life your Spirit will help me endure and keep my eyes fixed upon Jesus. Amen

CHASING AFTER: AUTHENTIC WORSHIP

Sam Hargreaves

More and more people are excited about
'worship'. CDs are selling, festivals are buzzing
with new songs and young people are pursuing
callings and even careers as worship leaders. I'm
excited about the passion I see in young people -
for God and for music and lifestyles that honour
him. But here's my plea and my prayer: let's go
above and beyond the notions of 'success' that
the world gives us. Let's reach higher and
deeper than previous generations, showing the

world what *real, authentic* worship is about.
What might that look like? Here are a few
sketches:

The young worship leader who is as
excited about engaging OAPs in worship
at the local residential home, or children
in an assembly, as he would be at leading
at a festival.

The young worship songwriter who writes
creative, challenging and singable songs
to serve her local community, regardless
of whether it tops the CCLI chart.

'Worship leaders' who use and encourage
all kinds of gifts: dance, drama, visuals,
poetry, DJing, craft... and more, to draw
new people in and approach God in fresh
ways.

Congregations inspired by the worship of
the persecuted and financially poor
church across the world, learning from
their spiritual riches and joining in their
cries.

Chasing After: Authentic Worship

 'Times of worship' that end up in places of confession, intercession, lament and action as often as they end up in intimacy and adoration; when we meet with God, it changes us.

 Young people uncovering riches from our 2000-year old Christian worship heritage, blowing off the dust, re-mixing the best and bringing it alive for 21st century disciples.

 Worship that dares to step out of comfortable answers to ask hard questions; embracing those with doubts, disappointments and depressions in the arms of a welcoming church.

 Missional worship that pushes to the edges of society; embracing new forms, music styles and patterns of being that allow the gospel to flower in deserts and housing estates.

Will it sell? Probably not. Will it be easy? Highly unlikely. Will it bring God's Kingdom come and his will be done, on earth as it is in heaven?

The Pursuit

Just maybe. Will it glorify his name and put a smile on his face? Undoubtedly.

5.

the pursuit of...

KINDNESS

Key Verse: Colossians 3:12

Since God chose you to be the holy people he loves, you must clothe yourselves with tenderhearted mercy, kindness, humility, gentleness, and patience.

The Pursuit

I don't know about you but I have a real
fascination with people-watching. Now before you
start to worry I'm not talking about hiding in the
bushes outside people's houses watching them
through the window, I believe that is called
stalking. I'm talking about those spare few
moments you have waiting for someone in a
restaurant or sitting on the train where you find
yourself observing the people around you. I wish
Sir David Attenborough would make a
documentary about us, curious creatures, with
the same attention to detail as he looks at the
world's other species. For my money we are the
most fascinating beings to observe on the planet.

I was recently sitting in an airport with some
time on my hands. After exhausting a less than
thrilling edition of Rolling Stone magazine
(there's only so long a feature on Polish folk
music will keep me entertained) my attention
turned to the various people around me in the
departures lounge. Airports are incredible places
for a quality dose of people-watching, with every
demographic and social group potentially
represented. Looking around the room you could
observe flustered parents trying to reign in
hyped-up children (E numbers before a flight are
a huge error), couples, young and old, flying to

and from romantic breaks, businessmen making last minute phone calls before losing their communication with the world for a few hours.

I couldn't help but wonder, as I sat there, where everyone was going, I mean, I had a vague idea of where they were traveling to that day, you could guess that much from reading the departures boards! But where were they going in life? That's what interests me most about watching people, that every single person is different, leading a different existence. Different lives, hopes and dreams, ambitions and passions, I could go on and on. Watching someone may give me a tiny insight into their life for that specific moment but it could never truly give me access to who they are.

The scary thing about observing people in such a way is when you turn it around on yourself. I wonder what other 'people-watchers' made of me as I was sitting there! What conclusions do they draw as they see me for these brief moments?

These days, airports are all about identity. Knowledge of identity is how we monitor security. Our passports give access to enough information about us to get from one country to another. When we arrive in a foreign nation we are asked for more information, most immediately, about

The Pursuit

Deeper Reading:

Psa 145:17

2 Cor 6:6

1 Pet 5:10

Eph 1:7

the intentions of our visit; business or pleasure. If you are really lucky you might even get taken into a side-room for further 'questioning', like my mate Andy, who must have a face that looks suspicious, as it happens every time we travel. Either that or he has a criminal record I don't know about, which would explain a lot, now that I think about it.

Although considered proof of our identity, to the average person, our passports give little more knowledge of who we are than 'people-watching' does. Sure, we can get a few key facts, but can we learn about the heart and desires of a person from their passport? The point is, sometimes in life we only have limited opportunity and circumstances to make an impression. In fact, when you think about it, our existence on this earth is so short, relative to all of time, that we really do only have a brief opportunity to leave a mark!

Could it ever be possible for a 'people-watcher' to spot me from across a busy airport and know that Jesus was the centre of my life, just by observing me for a short while? Wouldn't that be incredible?!

I shouldn't imagine there are too many people that wouldn't like to be known as a kind person. There is something about a simple act of kindness that can have a transforming effect on the person who benefits from it. I can think of numerous times in my life when I have been blessed by acts of kindness from other people, both large and small.

I took my first year out with British Youth For Christ straight from college, when I was 18 years old. One night my team gathered together for a Bible study that a couple of the girls had organised on the fruit of the Spirit (maybe that's where the origins of this book can be traced back to, in which case, thank you, Rachel and Anna!). They prepared a bowl of fresh fruit for the session and, as they talked through the nine aspects of the fruit of the Spirit, they would identify one member of the team who fit that fruit and then hand them a real fruit as a representation. I know what you're thinking, so-far-so-nice and creative Bible study. When it finally came around to the fruit they had identified me with, it turned out to be kindness. I remember for some reason being a little bit disappointed with that at the time. I think, as an 18 year old lad, the idea of being known as the kind one wasn't massively rock and roll! I guess I would have preferred the fruit of the rave or something equally irreverent and non-existent. Now that I look back on it, though, I can't help but smile. There surely can't be many other compliments as high as someone identifying you as being kind, especially at a spiritual level! I hope, if we were to do the study again today, that I would still come out with the same result (although strictly speaking we should be going for the whole bowl, rather than just one or two fruits from it!).

It's no coincidence that recent national Christian social action movements in the UK have been based around donating 'hours of kindness' instead of donating something like cash. It seems that in our sometimes faceless and individualistic society, kindness can be even more of a valuable asset than money and it is definitely a great opportunity for evangelism. Acts of kindness can see previously closed doors opened, cold hearts warmed, stubborn attitudes softened and, as with the other fruits (spot the running theme!), lives transformed.

Kindness

Simple (or complicated for that matter) acts of kindness are fantastic but they have to be born out of a lifestyle. The world doesn't simply need kind gestures; the world needs spiritually kind (and aware) people who will make an authentic impact through their actions and lifestyles. For kindness to really come out of my life in a world-changing way I have to allow Jesus to take his rightful place at the centre of it. That means more than just accepting him into your life, it means allowing God to influence all that you are. Not to become a Christian robot or clone. Far from it! This is to enter into the fullness of life as God intends it, with him as our centre.

It is also about grace. We have received so much grace from the Father, through what the Son has done, that for us to go on and reveal this to the world through the Spirit (of kindness) in our lives should be a no brainer! I haven't got space here to really unpack the grace aspect in all its gory detail, I'll have to save that for another day (or book!), but I will offer two quick thoughts.

First of all, grace is easy to abuse. The grace that we receive from God should never be taken lightly. It is not a get out of jail free card. 'I can do what I want because God is gracious and will forgive me', is just about as wrong an attitude as you could have. Grace does *not* make our sin acceptable! Grace makes it possible for sinners to be accepted through forgiveness. BIG difference. If you abuse grace in your life you will never enter into the fullness of relationship with Jesus that he desires to have with you. You will be like a groupie waiting at the gig door only catching glimpses of the band, instead of partying with them backstage. You will also compromise your ability to offer graciousness to others because the way you react to God will always impact the way you react to the world around you.

The Bible is very clear in speaking against that kind of thinking,

> *"I say this because some ungodly people have wormed their way into your churches, saying that God's marvellous grace allows us to live immoral lives. The condemnation of such people was recorded long ago, for they have denied our only Master and Lord, Jesus Christ."* (Jude 1:4)

This passage is saying that people who treat grace in such a way live lives that disregard Jesus and push him from his rightful place! That's pretty strong language but the message is clear; we must fight against such treatment of God's grace and hold strong to our faith. Paul makes it clear, in Ephesians 1, just what God's grace has done for us and puts Jesus back into the spotlight,

"He is so rich in kindness and grace that he purchased our freedom with the blood of his Son and forgave our sins." (Ephesians 1:7)

Reality check: you are a human being, therefore, you are not perfect. There will be times in your life that you will need to come before God and ask forgiveness and receive his grace. Never take this lightly, though, because the cost to God on the cross, whilst gladly paid for us all, was great. In the same way that we looked at the pursuit of love coming with a cost, so does grace. Do you see how it all comes together like a perfectly assembled jigsaw? (Perhaps with the cost of grace in mind you could go back and look at the pursuit of love again.)

Secondly, sometimes being gracious is the hardest thing in the world! There will be times in your life when the last thing you will want to do is show grace to someone, and yet, God is calling us all to a standard of living that is full of grace, full of kindness. We have been forgiven for the wrong things in our lives and, as Paul reminds us above, have had our debt paid for by the blood of Jesus, so how dare we not forgive those who do wrong to us in return! Sometimes (perhaps even often) easier said than done but if *we* can't reveal something of God's grace and forgiveness to the world, having ourselves already received so much from him, what hope do they have? And there is a truly Godly word - Hope. You don't have to look far in this world to see people living in hopelessness. This is one of the greatest tragedies of human existence, and here is why. When Jesus took our sin on the cross, he took all of the hopelessness of the world upon himself with it. Because of this we need never feel hopeless again, ever. Isn't that amazing? Yet we do see hopelessness around us in this world. Perhaps you are still experiencing some sense of hopelessness in your life today. Know that God's grace, his kindness towards us through Christ's sacrifice, can wipe that hopelessness away forever.

The amazing and exciting thing is that when we start living in a way that reveals grace and kindness, our identities will become so much more than just the sum of our hopes, dreams and ambitions. They will develop beyond our passions, our strengths and weaknesses, our achievements and failures. If God is at the centre of my identity, filling me with a spirit of kindness and a gracious heart, then my life becomes a living form of evangelism that can reveal hope to the hopeless. Christian evangelist and author Leonard Ravenhill quite rightly notes that,

"Any method of evangelism will work, if God is in it."

Whatever the method may be as you seek

to make the name of Jesus known, I pray that God is present in your life in such a way that you impact lives overwhelmingly with a living example of grace and kindness, the kind of life that someone will notice even from a distance.

Next time I am in a situation where I might be being 'people-watched', I hope I have no idea it's happening. I pray that whoever is watching sees something that makes them stop watching and start wondering.

Summary

- *Kind hearts and actions are cherished in this world.*

- *Do not abuse grace. Instead, be humbled by what you have received from God, and offer it to the world around you.*

- *We can become living forms of evangelism through lifestyles of kindness and grace.*

Questions

1. *What is Kindness?*

2. *What is the danger of abusing grace?*

3. *How can we reveal grace and kindness to the world?*

4. *How might people 'see' Jesus in your life?*

85

Challenge

Why don't you try and impact your local community through organised acts of kindness? Don't wait for a big organisation to spearhead something in your area, make it happen yourself! Put a team of friends together who will all be prepared to selflessly serve. There will be numerous charities in your area who will be looking for volunteers. You could distribute kindness vouchers that people could exchange for gardening work, help around the house. someone to do the shopping or whatever ideas you can come up with! Get out into your community and get creative with your time!

Prayer

Lord God, I am so humbled by the grace I have received from you. If I have ever taken for granted or abused your grace, I seek forgiveness now. May my heart be filled with kindness towards even those who sin against me. I ask your Spirit to help me to reveal your grace to the world and to live in a way which even a stranger is intrigued by. For your glory and honour. Amen

CHASING AFTER:
POLITICS AS MISSION

Andy Flanagan

So, I'm praying and asking God to reveal what He wants to bring to pass in the realm of politics. I feel an ever so kind kick-up the backside as I realise that he already has. He has planted this stuff inside many people the length and breadth of this country. As church members have encountered poverty and dysfunction during community action or international trips, their natural curiosity has led them to ask, "Why are things the way they are?" They're not satisfied by the status quo. They're not satisfied with mere charity that allows us to feel we've done the right thing, without effecting long-term change. In the words of Martin Luther King, they realise many before them have been content to just be the Good Samaritan on life's roadside but they want to improve the security of the Jericho Road so that no-one else gets mugged. Having heard so often the adolescent cry of, "It's not fair!" they're learning that injustice is often structural as well as personal. They're learning that until the global economic system is rewired according to principles of justice, rather than being ruled by the wealthy, any help we bring is quickly reversed. These facts are leading them to the natural conclusion things won't change while Christians are just shouting about them from the sidelines, rather than getting on the pitch.

Politics is just people serving people. For a Christian nothing should be more natural. I stood as a candidate for a by-election in my local area last year and as I knocked on people's doors and heard their stories, I realised that there was no one else knocking on these people's doors. No one else was allowing them to feel connected to the bigger picture. To be honest, I wouldn't have been there if I wasn't looking for their vote. The imperfect, yet brilliant thing that is democracy suddenly showed its worth as the glue that holds society together.

I write this from the midst of Labour HQ, so my glasses are not rose-tinted; this is not I dreaming, but genuine vision. God has promised to redeem and restore all of creation, and politics is merely the way we organise ourselves in the midst of it. God's perfection IS the future. It will happen. The only question is how soon. You can be certain that we're the ones who will be the limiting factor, not God. Yet, we have the privilege of being partners with Him in His project of "making all things new".

So here we go. In 2020...

Churches are missional in their DNA. People are continually serving their communities. They understand that this is a vital part of the discipleship deal, rather than a fun summer extra. Engagement with friends and community is breaking their hearts and forcing them to their knees. It's also highlighting where broken lives are a product of a broken society, so action is required not simply to mend individual lives, but to mend the context in which they attempt to grow.

The Pursuit

Young people are at the leading edge of an eschatological shift that has spread to the whole church. They see themselves as partners in God's restoration and redemption of all things as well as agents of the kingdom in the here and now. At gatherings people are commissioned to bring heaven on earth, rather than cajoled into buying an escape ticket for heaven. They're ruthless in their desire for justice and righteousness to burst forth in schools, supermarkets, youth clubs and the Internet. They refuse the old "EITHER/OR" of denominational or ecclesiological boundaries in favour of "BOTH/AND". They are just as comfortable lobbying a supermarket to stock fairly traded goods as they are praying for miraculous healings. And just as comfortable speaking in the town hall as a local councillor as they are speaking in tongues in a brightly coloured prayer room.

Local Conservative, Liberal Democrat, Green and Labour branches are flooded with young Christians who always hold the kingdom above any political ideology, yet realise the need to find common cause, to engage and debate. They refuse to make it about personality or abuse people and they make their case on the doorstep with a smile and a listening ear. People can see evidence of "the yeast working through the dough," because there is a renewed integrity and enthusiasm about politics.

It is as normal for a Christian young person to be pursuing a life in politics, as it is for them to aspire to being a worship leader. This calling is being affirmed and given space to grow. People are astounded that MPs are giving away so much of their money to good causes. The days when they were claiming expenses for garden gnomes are long forgotten.

So how could this have come to pass?

Everything shifted when we were encouraged to see politics as mission. When we put politics in that part of our brains and hearts, we started to understand. In the same way that we would encourage, pray for, emulate, visit and support a "missionary", we began to act like that towards those whose mission field was politics. Things changed when politics was presented as something exciting, counter cultural, and subversive rather than the maintenance of the "establishment."

Just people serving people rather than themselves.

6.
the pursuit
of...
GOODNESS

Key Verses: Luke 6:43-45

A good tree can't produce bad fruit, and a bad tree can't produce good fruit. A tree is identified by its fruit. Figs are never gathered from thorn bushes, and grapes are not picked from bramble bushes. A good person produces good things from the treasury of a good heart, and an evil person produces evil things from the treasury of an evil heart. What you say flows from what is in your heart.

When I was at school I was fortunate enough to escape without any real bullying issues. I'd love to say that the reason for this was that if I ever got hassled, then in true Bruce Lee style, I would open up a can of whoopage on the bully, liberate the school from their evil tyrannous reign and whisk the girl off into the sunset! But I would of course be telling porky pies. Sadly, I was no martial arts expert (although I should have been from the amount of times I watched The Karate Kid), and by the time I had the courage to talk to the girl, the sun had already set. But I did have one weapon in my arsenal against any potential bullies, comedy! It's amazing what situations you can get yourself out of when you have a bit of humour about you (mind you, it's amazing the situations you can get yourself into). So, thanks largely to the gift of the gab (and an older sister who had some rather tough friends) I had a pretty smooth ride. However, there are many who aren't so fortunate. Indeed, maybe as you read this now you are thinking of your own circumstances. I don't have any statistics about bullying to give you (you could call me lazy for not getting any but then I could accuse you of bullying!) but I'm sure if I did they would make for grim reading.

Goodness

Let me point out at this stage that I'm not just referring to playground bullying, which the majority of us most readily picture when the word bullying comes up. Bullying takes all sorts of shapes and forms and can affect any demographic, in any situation. School, work, home, relationships and family life; the list of bullying situations and environments can go on and on. It is just one form of injustice that plagues the world and affects far too many people on a daily basis.

As a Christian, my reaction to injustice in the world (big or small!) should be simple. It should make me angry. Not the anger that comes from personal grievance (selfish or hateful anger) but a selfless and righteous anger, so don't be passing that road rage off as righteous anger!

I used to love watching the old 'Incredible Hulk' TV show every Saturday night (you might be more familiar with one of the movies). Each week David Banner would travel to a new place and get involved in an unjust situation which, ultimately led to him transforming into a big green giant (fortunately not the same one as the peas and sweetcorn green giant, or there would have been havoc on the farm). He would then fight against the wicked to win victory for the oppressed. David Banner transforming into the

The Pursuit

Deeper Reading:

Jer 9:24

2 Thes 1:11-12

Psa 31:19

2 Pet 1:2-8

Eph 5:8-11

Hulk was the physical embodiment of his anger. I'm sure we've all been in situations where having that ability would have been useful, although the cost of the ripping shirts would soon mount up. But, as Christians, aren't we supposed to be loving and kind and...well, yes, of course! But the same kind of righteous (and indeed selfless) anger saw Jesus overturn the tables in the temple courtyard (Matthew 21:12-13). Jesus set the example for us that righteous anger should always be pro-active anger. This is definitely a good time to say that doesn't mean wanton destruction and damage or violent acts! It means appropriate action to the situation. This could manifest itself as speaking up to a teacher or parent about a problem, telling your boss about a situation, signing a petition or organising a demonstration (peaceful, please, and don't go covering yourself in green body paint for added 'Hulk' effect). Often times, speaking out publicly to the right people is the best outlet for our righteous anger.

How many times have you heard God referred to as 'good'? If you've ever sung a worship song in church I'm sure those words will have come from your own mouth. The Bible definitely presents the idea that God is good. The Psalms, for example, are full of such declarations, Psalm 116:5 says,

"How kind the Lord is! **How good he is!** *So merciful, this God of ours!"*

So it stands to reason that, if we are to adopt the fruit of the Spirit in our lives, and if the fruit are kind of like God's spiritual DNA, then somewhere along the line we must ourselves become 'good'!

But what does goodness look like in action? Well, in case you haven't already connected the dots from the first part of this chapter, goodness goes hand in hand with justice. We need to be a people of justice and righteousness.

When something is stirred in your heart do something about it! Some of the worst things that have happened to people (by people) occurred because no one spoke out, no one acted.

The Pursuit

We cannot account for the world's actions. Christians cannot even account for other Christians' actions. But we can account for our own individual actions. As we, one by one, begin to act and speak out against injustice in this world, big and small, so we may encourage one another, Christian or not, to do the same. You don't have to believe in Jesus to benefit from his example. Remember, goodness is not a concept limited to Christianity; but we should never forget that only God is truly and completely good.

A question I am often asked in Q&A sessions is: If we are made in the image of God, and yet are capable of doing bad things, does that mean there is bad in God as well as good? The easy answer to that question is 'no,' and I use this simple (widely-used - I do not claim it as my own) illustration to explain it.

Does darkness exist? Scientifically speaking, no it does not. Darkness, unmeasurable, is simply the result of an absence of light, which is measurable. If God is all that is good (light), and you remove him from the situation, what are you left with? God has no evil in him; there is nothing bad about him whatsoever. He is wonderfully and perfectly good! The problems come when we sideline God in this world. The more we push him to the margins of

REMIX:

"One can give without loving, but one cannot love without giving." This is a quote from the biography of Amy Carmichael. What can you learn from her life's service to God about living a life of goodness even in the face of personal struggle?

our lives, the more darkness we are left with as a result. But, when we choose to stand up for justice and righteousness, when we keep God as the centre of our moral compass and lives, His goodness can overcome the darkness.

If you are reading this, thinking that the challenge of this pursuit is simply about donating a few hours a month to a charity fighting for some form of justice, you are very wrong! Like all of these aspects of the fruit of the Spirit, it demands an actual response to God, and a change of lifestyle. In this case, for us to genuinely grow in spiritual goodness we also need to be willing to live a life of purity.

A spiritually good heart must be full of light. When we allow darkness in we reduce our capacity and our desire for goodness. For instance, filling our minds with unhelpful imagery, like sexual or excessively violent material, to name just two examples, usually serves no purpose other than for our own gratification and yet can be very damaging. I don't want to sound like a prude (or a dietician) but what you put in will always affect what comes out.

It's a bit like trying to drive a car when you have filled the petrol tank half with petrol and half with chocolate milkshake. As tasty as the chocolate milkshake may be, it is of no use as fuel to the car and will actually damage the engine over time, meaning you will eventually break down. I'm not saying you shouldn't ever watch TV or go to the cinema, or anything like that, just that you should think about the fuel that you feed your heart and you mind on. Fill your heart with purity, light and the goodness of God and you will be better fuelled to live a life that reflects his goodness in all that you do. And, more importantly, all that you are.

If there is injustice in the world, it is because we allow it to exist. I pray that we all have the courage and sense of justice to help speak out and stand up for and alongside those who need us. I pray you will be there for me when I have no voice and I ask forgiveness from God and from anyone who has ever suffered injustice where I failed to speak up.

Goodness

David Banner would always say, just before he turned big and green, "You wouldn't like me when I'm angry". And, sure enough, they never did! When acting with the spirit of goodness present in our lives, and with a pure heart, the world needs us when we're angry.

Summary

- *God is good!*

- *We should stand up against injustice, and be a voice for the voiceless.*

- *God desires for us to have pure hearts, fuel for his goodness to shine in our lives.*

Questions

1. *How do you know that God is good?*

2. *What kind of things stir up a righteous anger in you?*

3. *Why do you think purity is so important to spiritual goodness?*

4. *How can the church stand up for justice in this world? What role can you play?*

Challenge

If you want a spiritually good heart, you need to feed it the right things. Set yourself a spiritual diet for a month to start the process of healthier spiritual living. Are there some things (like in all good diets) that you maybe need to cut back on, or cut out altogether?

Exercise plays a roll in most diet strategies, so what are you going to take up that will spiritually tone you up! Maybe lose 30 mins of TV a day and gain 30 mins of Bible time? Also, I have more success going to the gym for real when I go with a friend. Apply the same idea here and help get each other in to peak spiritual condition!

Prayer

Father God you are good. I am sorry, Lord, that I do not always live in a way that shows your goodness to others. Help me maintain a pure heart and be wise about how I fuel my heart, mind and soul. Give me the confidence and wisdom to stand up for justice, and in so doing, reflect something of your goodness so that the world may be changed by it. In the name of Jesus. Amen.

CHASING AFTER:

JUSTICE

Ben Cooley

Rachel[1] was just fifteen when both her parents died. When someone at her church offered her a job and a new life in the UK she was grateful for the opportunity. She left her home in West Africa and arrived in England hoping to build a better future. Two months later after being abused and forced to work as a prostitute in a brothel on the South Coast, she managed to escape and find her way to a police station. She still lives in fear that the traffickers will find her. This isn't fiction, it's not the latest Hollywood film, it is the cold, harsh reality of

---

[1] Name changed to protect identity

trafficking in the UK. There are thousands of Rachels in towns and cities across this nation but you will not hear their stories, because they haven't escaped or been rescued. They are still being held against their will and sold for sex.

The statistics are shocking, children as young as three are being trafficked into the UK for sex, drugs and domestic slavery[2], and 99 per cent of victims are never rescued[3].

God places value on every life, every woman, every girl whose life is being destroyed at the hands of traffickers. He knows their names, to Him they are not just a statistic, they are his precious daughters. It says in Psalm 72, 'He will rescue them from oppression and violence for precious is their blood in his sight'[4]. I passionately believe that as the church it is our responsibility and our call to fight trafficking. We need to place the same value on the lives of

---

[2] ECPAT UK Report

[3] ECPAT UK Report

[4] Psalm 72:14 (NIV)

every Rachel out there that He does, because that will compel us to act.

As Christians we are called to be the light of the world. Lights seem to shine more brightly in dark places. If we are to be light bringers then we must find darkness to shine in, not just stay at home admiring the light of the gospel. I can tell you working with Hope for Justice has shown me that the world of trafficked people is a very dark place full of brokenness, abuse and desperation. I am convinced that if Jesus walked the earth today he would be heading for those dark places to bring God's light and freedom. We need to be people that do more than listen to the gospel, we need to live it.

We the church have an answer to trafficking because God is on our side. David was a young boy who stood and faced Goliath because he knew God was with him. He got angry at the injustice of what was happening and said, 'Who is this Philistine anyway that he is allowed to defy the armies of the living God'[5]. It's time for the church to unite against trafficking

---

[5] 1 Samuel 17:26 (NIV)

and do the same, to say 'who is this trafficker anyway that they are allowed to take our children and rape them for profit! NOT on our watch!'. When we step out in faith God steps into situations and does what we can't. He helps us slay Goliath, so what are we waiting for?

Trafficking is a massive issue, there is no quick fix or easy answer to it. It will take long obedience in the same direction to end slavery. I believe all it will take is one generation to stand for justice on the earth, who are passionate about making a difference. Why not us, why not now? Together we can be the ones to bring God's hope and justice to the Rachels of this world.

7.
the pursuit of...
FAITHFULNESS

Key Verse: John 1:17

For the law was given through Moses,

but God's unfailing love

and faithfulness came through

Jesus Christ.

The Pursuit

As a football fan of both club (Leeds United, don't hold it against me) and country I've had my fair share of ups and downs, highs and lows and flat out heartbreak! I remember with a pained nostalgia one final that particularly hurt, as Leeds were beaten 3-0 on a rather gloomy and depressing afternoon. My strongest memory of the game is how badly we played. After showing so much promise all season, the team we knew failed to show up and play as they could.

Have you ever had one of those days at school, college or work where you just don't feel like you're quite with it? I had a good five years of that feeling through secondary school! A friend of mine at school totally messed up one of his GCSE exams because on the day, mentally, he just didn't turn up. Isn't it frustrating how we can let ourselves, and others, down by not 'showing up' and giving it our all at times?

The phenomenal rise of social networking means that, to a certain extent, everyone knows what everyone else is doing and feeling all of the time. Keeping your status updated with your latest movements (not appreciated if you have irritable bowel syndrome), or Tweeting your current emotional state of mind, is par for the course in the modern online world. For the most part, it can be pretty boring stuff, but recently a friend's status update caught my eye, saying the following,

> *"Church was amazing today, God showed up!"*

What an amazingly strange thing to say. How can a God, who is always present everywhere (omnipresent) show up? Surely that would be like me trying to physically show up to myself, which is impossible, of course, as I am always with me, as is God, for that matter.

My buddy, Mark, who is a teacher, was telling me recently about a stint he did working at a Christian school. Being a church-based school they would meet for a formal chapel-type assembly once a week. This service was taken very seriously, as God himself would be present; a fact that was shown with a red light on the wall. When the light was on, God was in the house. When the light was off God was elsewhere, presumably practising his golf putt in his heavenly office, between earthly appearances.

I can just imagine the kids shuffling into the chapel before a hushed silence creeps across the room, all eyes fixed on the light. And then, 'ping'; God is among us! I hope access to the switch was limited. A trigger-happy renegade could cause havoc at weekly chapel with God forced to pop in and out of the service at the flick of a switch.

This line of thinking is, quite frankly, a bit silly. Now, before you start accusing me of being picky over a harmless statement or needlessly attacking the observation of a reverent tradition, let me say there is a very good reason why such thinking should be challenged.

Church, for many, has become an experience, something we do on a Sunday morning as a part (and for some people it makes up all) of our Christian lives. More so it has become an experience we seek to benefit from, get topped up by, or shudder at the thought, enjoy. Now, joking aside, you should absolutely be able to benefit from, be refreshed by and indeed enjoy church (by which, from here on, I refer mainly to the group gatherings). But equally and importantly, it's okay if you don't! Not everything at your Sunday (or any other day) meetings will float your boat. You might find one week boring, the next electric. One act of worship may move us to tears of joy, another breaks our hearts whilst another leaves us without emotion.

The problem creeps in when we evaluate our worship experiences (and even our actual *relationship* with God) based on whether God 'shows up', more often than not meaning; did I

Deeper Reading:

Prov 14:22

Hab 2:4

Lam 3:23

John 1:14

engage with it? Did I enjoy it? Was I satisfied by my experience? All *me* questions. If I got into it then God showed up. If I didn't he must have had the morning off! Then again there are the times when 'God showing up' is used to describe a more visual working of the Holy Spirit among us. Sure there are times when the Spirit of God might be more obviously present but is He ever actually more or less present? Of course not!!

God NEVER fails to show up. NEVER. It is us who clock in and out on God, picking and choosing when we want to opt in or out of his presence and worship as it suits our lives. It says so much about our walk with Christ when we use such terminology as 'God showing up', to evaluate, even excuse, our effort or lack thereof; our highs and lows, our pleasure and pain, our pride and shame. God longs for us to show up, as we are, to the place where he is always, and to choose to worship him.

It is about faithfulness. God is always

faithful to us; it is a fundamental aspect of who he is! Look at what these Psalms have to say about God's faithfulness:

"But you, O Lord, are a God of compassion and mercy, slow to get angry and filled with unfailing love and faithfulness." (Psalm 86:15)

"Your unfailing love will last forever. Your faithfulness is as enduring as the heavens." (Psalm 89:2)

"For the Lord is good. His unfailing love continues forever, and his faithfulness continues to each generation." (Psalm 100:5)

Notice the link between God's love and his faithfulness? Check out the key verse for the pursuit of faithfulness. It is one of the most significant verses in all of the Bible! Jesus is the physical embodiment of God's love and faithfulness! We should be in no doubt that God loves us and we can live in the truth that he will never let us down. He is completely faithful!

It is we who let God down. It is our

faithfulness that is in question. Sadly our faithfulness to God too often comes down to how we are 'feeling' at any specific moment; but God wants *all* of you, *all* of the time. Complete commitment, complete obedience, complete faithfulness, in the good times and the bad.

Faithfulness also requires that we live with integrity, which can best be described as living consistently within the values that God has set for us. When I first started out in Christian ministry many years ago someone advised me that one of the most important things I could have in ministry was

REMIX:

How much faithfulness did surf champion Bethany Hamilton show in the wake of losing her arm in a shark attack? Check out the movie 'Soul Surfer' (2011) and do some research online to find out more.

integrity. It makes sense as living with integrity helps move us away from living lives of hypocrisy and demonstrates, both to God and to the world, that we are prepared to live for greater things no matter what the personal cost.

Next time you're in a church gathering I

challenge you to show up! Regardless of how you feel, how your week has been or is looking like ahead. No matter how much sleep you got the night before, no matter how frustrated you are about the previous day's football scores! Show up and choose to worship and, whether it is the best worship experience of your life, or the worst (which begs the question of how you evaluate your worship), know that God is always with you, always faithful and longing for you to 'show up'. Then rise to the challenge fully and take that attitude of faithfulness beyond just your Christian gatherings and into every area of your life!

I want to give all of my heart to God, to let those gatherings be an extension of the day-to-day of my week and church community, so that, no matter what day I were to check out God's status update, I could read his words of joy,

"Amazing day today. Ben showed up."

Summary

- *God is always with us, always present.*

- *God has demonstrated his faithfulness and love perfectly through Jesus.*

- *We must chose to 'show up' no matter how we are feeling, as God is calling us to live faithfully and with integrity.*

Questions

1. *How has God demonstrated His faithfulness in your life?*

2. *What are the areas of your life in which you struggle to be faithful to God?*

3. *How can you live with integrity?*

4. *What could it mean in your life to always choose to 'show up' for God?*

Challenge

Think of someone you know who does not yet know Jesus. Got the name? Good, because you are now going to pray for that person every day! No exceptions, make sure you always offer that person in prayer to God. Faithfulness in prayer is a really important part of our relationship with God, and using it to pray specifically for the lost demonstrates we share God's heart. Honour God with faithfulness in this way and he will honour you!

Prayer

Faithful God, thank you for your unfailing love. I am sorry for the times when I do not live faithfully for you. Thank you that you will never let me down, and that you are always with me. I want to rise to the challenge of living with integrity and always 'showing up' for you, no matter how I'm feeling. In Jesus' almighty name. Amen.

CHASING AFTER:
THE IMAGE
OF GOD

Riley Armstrong

I used to think that being made in the image of God meant He had arms and legs like me. In fact, I still remember the morning in church that my Sunday school teacher told me He didn't - and I was appalled. I remember after the lesson, conversing with my young primary school buddy that this teacher must have taken crazy pills because it just seemed so very obvious

that being made in His image meant having arms
and legs! Thinking back to that time in my life
now as an adult, it makes sense that I would
think that. I mean arms and legs are really what
the life of being a boy is all about. Running,
kicking, building, punching... you know, boy stuff.
It was later in adolescence that I opened up to
considering that, okay... maybe God didn't look
like me. It probably was an incredibly baffling
passage like John 1 ("In the beginning was the
Word . . . and the Word was God . . .") that I
didn't really understand, and yet helped me
realise that there was more to this image of God
thing than I had initially thought.

Biology class was one of those classes that
you had to take in the tenth grade. You could opt
out in grade eleven but everyone had to take that
first year. I had heard the stories of dissecting
earth worms and cow eyes and it totally freaked
me out. My childhood was an anomaly. I had
grown up on a farm in Northern Canada but had
an aversion to gross things. By gross things I
mean just about all living organisms that aren't a
friendly dog or a mild-mannered cat. I remember
turning off the lawn tractor while mowing the
yard and running to the house to get rubber
gloves from under the kitchen sink, for there was
a frog in the way of the mower... and I needed to

move it! You can see why the thought of having to touch and examine a pickled creature alongside my 'eager to start chopping things up' peers didn't thrill me. The thought of it even to this day makes me hyper-ventilate a little!

However, it was in this class that we learned much about the incredibly complex and mind-blowing world of life all around us. I remember the teacher telling us that planet earth and all natural things on it were carbon-based, including us humans. That was interesting. It sure lined up with God making us from earth, for example, since dirt is carbon-based.

So, then, what makes us any different than dirt? That's easy, we're alive and breathing. Okay then, what makes us any different than, say, a horse? My Bio class would have deduced that we have many things in common, and we do; more than just having carbon in our fibres. Yet there is still a massive ball of obvious physical differences! When we set even these aside, we are left with what I believe are some amazing and special things to being human, and at this point I believe we are getting a whole lot closer to what it means to be made in the image of God.

The Pursuit

An animal will live and die, communicate, feel pain, learn, raise young, have blood pumping through veins, just like us, to name a few of the more complex similarities. But then we quickly edge into those differences between animals and humanity that are far more than biological. Now we can begin to see something substantially more valuable: what it really means to be human, as opposed to *any other* living thing. Here lies how we mirror our Creator. It lies in both the intangible - laughter, love, reason, compassion, righteousness and the ability to recognise beauty - but also in tangible things like creating, and designing; much like our Creator God has done in nature all around us. You don't need to look very far to see that not only did God use a crazy amount of colours when He got creative with planet earth, but He gave us the special ability to recognise and appreciate them as something beautiful.

Let me give you a few examples:

Have you ever watched a little baby laughing really hard which releases this amazing joy inside you and you find yourself laughing too?

Chasing After: The Image of God

How about a movie where the underdog defies all odds to win in the end, and you feel life bubble up from within you?

What about a song on the car stereo that you just can't turn up loud enough because it resonates with the very core of who you are?

Have you ever seen something tragic in the news that causes your heart to break a little for those involved and ignite a thirst for justice inside you?

These, my friends, are the internal fireworks of the image of God bursting through the thick skin of our existence to remind us that there is more to life that just being a human, more than just biology, more than just being dirt. There is a divine calling to mirror the Creator.

To create. To laugh. To love.

8.
the pursuit of...
GENTLENESS

Key Verses: Ephesians 4:2-6

Always be humble and gentle. Be patient with each other, making allowance for each other's faults because of your love. Make every effort to keep yourselves united in the Spirit, binding yourselves together with peace. For there is one body and one Spirit, just as you have been called to one glorious hope for the future. There is one Lord, one faith, one baptism, and one God and Father, who is over all and in all and living through all.

The Pursuit

I love those adverts on TV that ask us the question, "Have you been in an accident at home or work that wasn't your fault?" We always get some sort of true-life tale of how someone fell from a ladder at work, or someone who was run over by a fork-lift truck, or something equally unfortunate (doubly unfortunate if you fall off the ladder into the path of an oncoming fork-lift truck). I find them hilarious because they usually do a great job of finding the most uninspiring people on the planet to tell their story. I have never met anyone in real life quite as dull as these people are presented to be; I can only assume it's because they are all too busy falling off things and filming adverts. The point of the adverts, of course, is to inform us that we could get compensation for our troubles because, after all, where there's blame, there's a claim!

Such adverts are a sad reflection of an aggressive and responsibility-shirking culture that always looks to place the blame somewhere. How many times have we seen incidents recently in the media where someone's head must roll for their involvement in a mistake or scandal? The real problem with a blame and claim culture, though, is that more often than not we look to place responsibility anywhere except 'me'. The reality of that attitude is a society that merely shakes its head and points its finger.

Imagine that you told your best friend not to jump into a swimming pool because they couldn't swim but they did it anyway (sounds like something one of my friends would do). Sure, you'd be mad at them for not listening to you, so pointing the finger and shaking your head would convey that emotion to them, but it's not going to stop them from drowning.

Do you think God ever, even for a moment, thinks this world would be better without the people? We do, after all, cause so many problems! However, the Bible's account of Jesus' life, death and resurrection reveals the actions not of a God who points the finger and watches but of a God of compassion and mercy who dives in the deep end to show us how and make it possible for us to swim. Not only that but God made us all to swim in our own style (I'm a front-stroke man myself; butterfly is surely for show offs).

I recently heard someone make the beautifully, and intentionally, ironic statement,

"Church would be great without the people!"

It can certainly feel that way, sometimes. The problem with people is that we complicate

things with our feelings and emotions, our
individuality and conformity. We make group
situations difficult by having a voice or not having
one. We step on each other's toes with our
preferences, likes and dislikes. We complicate
community with the 'me' attitude. Sorry folks but
that's just the way it is. Community, and
therefore church, is people, and people are...
well... complicated.

It saddens me greatly to think on the many
church and community situations I am aware of
that have been broken or damaged by the 'blame
and claim' culture. It saddens me even more
when I think on the times when I have been
guilty of such an attitude, times where I have
been lacking in compassion. So many of these
problems are often less about 'wrongs' and more
about 'likes'. So often we allow ourselves to be
offended by people and situations that are not
about 'me' or 'for me' and yet we are so good at
making ourselves the focus. When we choose to
take offence the knock-on effect is that we must
place blame somewhere (anywhere except
numero-uno). We seek to take (claim) from
someone at a time when we should give, just as
God could have claimed from us for our wrongs
and offences and yet instead gave us Jesus. The
society-driven mix-up of claiming instead of

giving is the cause of so many of our problems.

Where has the compassion gone from our society? Where has the mercy gone from some of our churches? The blame and claim culture brings with it such an aggressive attitude, completely lacking in any compassion and mercy that we, as followers of Jesus, should be desperate to see the fruit of gentleness ripe in the church.

Deeper Reading:

Psa 51:1

Ex 34:6

Mat 11:29

Lu 10:30-37

It is important for me to point out that I am not suggesting we let true wrongs (and sins) go by without consequence. Far from it. Community cannot work in such a way. But, instead of looking to place blame, let us look at our own responsibilities, to ourselves, each other and, ultimately, to God who has laid down an example of mercy to us all through the cross.

During his Sermon on the Mount, Jesus says the following,

"God blesses those who are merciful, for they will be shown mercy." (Matthew 5:7)

The Pursuit

What are our expectations of each other? I may never set out to let anyone down. But, in my human existence, it is almost inevitable that I will. That is no excuse for getting things wrong but it is a basis, along with the example of Jesus, for understanding compassion (as we have already looked at in the pursuit of kindness and grace). Tolerance is not a word I hear often in the church these days and yet is crucial to a gentle heart. When we learn to become more tolerant of, and compassionate to, each other we will see our communities transformed.

I'm sure you are all familiar with the story of the Good Samaritan (see deeper reading). Short version: a Jewish man gets beaten up by bandits and left for dead on the side of the road. A few people you might expect to help walk by and ignore him but eventually a Samaritan man offers help, even though the Samaritans and the Jews are enemies! So why does the Samaritan help the Jew? Luke 10:33 explains it like this,

*"Then a despised Samaritan came along, and when he saw the man, he felt **compassion** for him."*

Spiritual compassion is strong enough to even overcome the barriers of the most hated of enemies! Powerful stuff, especially when you consider that we can sometimes fail to show compassion to those people that we actually like!

Now there is of course the kind of compassion that we pour out to the obviously needy of this world. Another staple kind of advert from the daytime TV schedule (I realise this is starting to sound like I just sit at home all day watching television) is what I refer to as the 'Just £2' ads. These are usually a plea for you to donate a small amount of money each week to aid a worthy humanitarian project of some variety (or for dogs who narrate their own advert which is very clever of them). Proactively getting involved in charitable projects which work with those in need or even financially supporting them is a great way to be compassionate to this world and to demonstrate God's own compassionate heart. But for many of us the challenge really begins at home, at school, at church, at work, with those around us day by day. Are you really living in a way that reveals God's mercy to those around you?

It can be all too easy to fall into the trap of thinking that you've done all you need to do because you give a few pounds each month to help feed some children in a third-world nation. If you only ever view compassion as something you do as a charitable act for those who seem to have an obvious and great need, you will never see true spiritual gentleness take root in your life. 'Doing' charitable acts is worthwhile and laudable, but 'being' compassionate and merciful in every area of our lives, to all we encounter personally *and* those we can impact from afar, is the goal for followers of Jesus.

A popular soundbite from one of those charitable adverts goes along the lines of,

"Give a man a fish and he can feed himself for a day, but give him the tools to fish and he can feed his family for a lifetime".

REMIX:

A quote I used in the first ever preach I did, and still often use today is, "If [a rose] is fragrant, people will walk across the garden and endure the thorns to smell it." This was spoken by Mahatma Gandhi to a group of Christian missionaries. What do you think he meant when he said this, and what can you learn from his life about gentleness and mercy?

Gentleness

You can apply this same model of thinking to underline why God expects more from us than just charitable acts,

"Do a charitable act and help the world for a day, but become spiritually compassionate and help this world for a lifetime"

By the power of His Spirit in your life, God wants to give you the tools to show gentleness, compassion and mercy to this world for as long as you live and breathe in it.

To milk the swimming pool metaphor for all its worth, we have been given the responsibility of being a 'life guard' to the world, and yet, too often, when we see people drowning, we do not have the compassion to jump in and get wet; possibly spending more time blowing our whistle and telling someone off for breaking the rules by running!

If we want the fruit of the Spirit to flow from our lives, we cannot subscribe to the 'where there's blame, there's a claim' culture. Because of Jesus, we are compelled to dive into the deep end and offer compassion and mercy, through the spirit of gentleness, to those who need it; no matter who they are, or how we may feel about them. The call is clear.

The Pursuit

"'Now which of these three would you say was a neighbour to the man who was attacked by bandits?' Jesus asked. The man replied, 'The one who showed him mercy.' Then Jesus said, "Yes, now go and do the same."'" (Luke 10:36-37)

Summary

- *Spiritual gentleness can be measured in our compassion and mercy to others.*

- *God blesses those who are merciful.*

- *Everyone is different. Although that can make showing compassion hard at times, we are called to share it even with our 'enemies'.*

Questions

1. *Where do you see gentleness and compassion in this world?*

2. *Why do you think God blesses those who are merciful?*

3. *How has God demonstrated his compassion and mercy to you?*

4. *What impact could you make in your community as God's spirit of gentleness flows from your life?*

Challenge

Why not take on the challenge of sponsoring a child? There are many fantastic organisations such as the aptly named Compassion who facilitate the sponsorship of children all around the world. You could make it a group activity with some friends and all chip in together. The genuine help you will be giving a needy child, combined with the connection you will have with your sponsor buddies will be a great grounding to tackle the more difficult areas of compassionate living, such as even being prepared to help a so called enemy!

www.compassionuk.org (UK)
www.compassion.com (US)

Prayer

Lord Jesus, I want to respond to your call to show compassion to all in need. I'm sorry that I let my own agenda get in the way sometimes. I pray that my life will reflect the gentleness of the Father, so that people may know his mercy. I pray for this with the help of your spirit. Amen.

CHASING AFTER:

THE AWESOME

Steve Gambill

Acts 11:19-26

Have you ever found something so amazing, so incredible and so awe-inspiring that you are desperate to tell all your friends about it? Have you ever seen an idyllic, paradise beach on television and thought I must visit there? Or perhaps you once heard a band so incredible that you were willing to pay big bucks to see them live in concert?

Early in my career, Disneyworld at Orlando Florida employed me. Like most people I found

Disney to be an amazing place. The Imagination, excellence and attention to detail made a great impact on me. The staff followed the dream of Walt Disney to 'create the happiest place on earth.'

When my contract finished and I returned to my local church in the Midwest of America, my eyes had been opened as to how average our approach was in certain areas. Even though my church was a good church, with some incredible people, there were many things that I 'put up with' that Disney would refuse to allow. I realized that I had been conditioned to accept things as they were. This realization led me to ask the question...

WHY DO I SETTLE FOR AVERAGE IN CHURCH LIFE WHEN GOD HAS AMAZING IN STORE FOR US?

It was and still is my conviction that the local church has been entrusted with the vital responsibility to reflect the amazing nature of God. Yet when I looked around my local setting and saw:

Buildings in poor condition. Walls scuffed in need of paint, stained carpets, broken lights.

Little creativity or innovation in programming resulting in predictable and sometimes boring meetings. Music of a very poor quality and substandard musicianship.

Not many people came, or even knew we existed in comparison to the amount of people that lived around our area.
Not many young people were interested in our local church programmes.

I realised that even though I wasn't a "leader" at the time, it was my responsibility to be part of the solution. I had just left Disney employment where most of the work force were young people like me, yet they were part of an amazing organisation. I feared that my neglect of initiative taking and acceptance of average could lead people to wrong conclusions about God. Though I felt inexperienced and inadequate, I began a quest to make God's house more amazing than the house of a rodent! This quest, led me to England and to pioneer a young peoples ministry in West Yorkshire. In launching Rocknations, I began to ask myself questions like "What will it take to make local church amazing? What will take to make youth ministry amazing?"

WHAT AMAZING MEANS

Amazing is an awesome word. Amazing literally means - extraordinary, wonderful, barely believable or to cause extreme surprise. It is my conviction that amazing is a word that should reflect everything associated with Jesus Christ. After all Jesus is God made flesh. Jesus is the innovative rescuer of humankind, who rose from the dead. Pretty amazing wouldn't you say so? Why is it that so many people, especially young people still find the local church (His reflection on the earth) boring dull and predictable? Wouldn't it be awesome if our youth meetings were summed up by extreme surprise?

GOD'S AMAZING IDEA – THE LOCAL CHURCH

The church was initiated by Jesus to be an amazing place on earth. Jesus declared (Mt 16:18) ...on this rock, I will build my church, and the gates of Hell will not overcome it. Jesus went on to say after His resurrection (Acts 1:8) But will receive power when the Holy Spirit comes on you, and you will be my witnesses in Jerusalem, Judea and to the ends of the earth. It didn't take long before strong local churches emerged in places like Corinth, Ephesus, Galatia and in many other places.

The incredible thing is that the leaders of the early church who were the custodians of this amazing plan were average ordinary people like you and me. Acts 4:13 states that when people saw the courage of Peter and John and realised that they were unschooled, ordinary men, they were astonished and they took note that these men had been with Jesus.

INVESTING QUALITY TIME WILL LEAD TO AMAZING RESULTS

Peter and Johns incredible exploits were not an accident, but rather the result of Jesus having invested quality time in them. That investment, later led to God doing incredible things through them. Spending quality time with Jesus and then investing your life in others is an absolute necessity in producing amazing results. In my early days as a youth pastor, older wiser people invested hours into my life. They challenged, provoked, questioned, and encouraged me all for which I am totally grateful. In turn, I would pour quality times into the teenagers around me.

The truth is, the more of Jesus we have in

our personal lives, the more amazing the local church will become. Eph 3:10 Reveals that Gods intent was that now through the church, the manifold wisdom of God should be made known to the rulers and authorities in the heavenly realms. If you need more wisdom, then the good news is that it is available to you in Christ.

Keep at it, keep loving, and keep serving over the long haul. Find the fatherless, search for those who are sick, always be on the lookout for the lost and when you find them, embrace and love them completely for decades and the results will speak for themselves.

9.
the pursuit of...
SELF DISCIPLINE

Key Verses: 2 Peter 1:5-7

In view of all this, make every effort to respond to God's promises. Supplement your faith with a generous provision of moral excellence, and moral excellence with knowledge, and knowledge with self-control, and self-control with patient endurance, and patient endurance with godliness, and godliness with brotherly affection, and brotherly affection with love for everyone.

The Pursuit

I used to have a DJ residency in a bar near where I lived. Three out of four Friday nights I would entertain a room full of drunken dancers, pretending to myself that at least some of them were impressed by my DJ skills (they weren't, they were too drunk).

There's something incredibly strange about being one of the few sober people in a room of 'happy' dancers. For a start, you get to see some insanely strange dancing, which under normal circumstances would surely be illegal. More than that, though, you can sometimes start to think that everyone is involved in a really great party, which you haven't been invited to. People look so free when they've knocked a few back. Have you ever heard anyone referred to as 'more fun after a few drinks'? After all it's not often the sober one at an evening with alcohol is remembered as the life and soul of the party.

A couple of years ago I decided to give up alcohol for a year. You might ask why? Did I have a problem? Was this some sort of overtly spiritual obligation? Was my dancing that bad? Why would I choose to give up something that I actually really enjoy?

The answer in this case was discipline. "DISCIPLINE?" I hear you cry! We get enough of that at school or college, at home, at work! That

Discipline

may be true, but this is a different kind of discipline. This is the kind of discipline that dares to say 'God, you are more important than me'.

We live in a culture now where people are encouraged to do what they want to do. So long as nobody else gets hurt feel free to get on with it. While you are still at the age where your parents have a good chunk of control over your life this can be especially frustrating and kids of a younger and younger age are now demanding a level of independence they would never have dreamed of even twenty years ago.

Well, I'm here to tell you that discipline is great! The older I get the more desperate I am to fall in line with the plan God has for my life. To do that, though, I have to give my life to him completely and that means living a life of discipline. It might sound boring but this isn't the kind of 'If you do that you'll be grounded!' discipline. No, this is where we *choose* to live a certain way in the knowledge that it will make our relationship with God stronger.

Let's go back to my drinking situation. I didn't have a 'problem' with alcohol (or dancing thank you very much!) and I certainly do not condone getting drunk at all. Nor did I experience the voice of God from a burning beer keg telling me to put an end to my drinking days!

The Pursuit

Deeper Reading:

1 Sam 2:30

Job 5:17

1 Cor 9:27

Deu 8:5

1 Thes 5:4-11

To set the scene more fully I was just about to begin a new phase of Christian ministry and I knew that it was going to be a real challenge. I looked at my life and decided that a few things needed to change. I needed to be more organised (I'm working on it) and I needed a little bit more discipline, discipline that would lead to less of me and more of God in my life. Giving up alcohol for a year seemed like something that could be challenging and sacrificial. It could have just as easily been chocolate, I guess, or television. But then again, maybe God chose alcohol for a very good reason after all.

Christmas is my favourite time of year (apart from the cold but apparently we get that in the summer now too) and I always look forward to the festivities. During my yearlong drinking break it was Christmas when I missed a little drink the most. Strange how this relatively small lifestyle change impacted one of the most significant moments of my year as a Christian.

Funny thing is every time I went to get a soft drink it was a little reminder of what I was doing and more importantly why and for who I was doing it. For the rest of that year every time I was in a bar or at a house party it was a conversation starter leading to some of the best God-centred conversations I had all year! God certainly knows me! By honouring him in this discipline he honoured me by giving me incredible opportunities for conversation and witness. In all the times I have ever been in a bar with a beer I have never been so frequently asked the questions I was asked without one!

Many of you reading this will not be legally old enough to purchase alcohol, and yet I'm fully aware that some of you will already be drinking, on occasion. Getting hold of alcohol is not the difficult thing for some of you; but learning to say 'no' and exercise some self-discipline when the opportunity arises is. Peer pressure is a challenge at any age and stage of your life (and extends far beyond the example of the mis-use of alcohol). But during your teenage years it seems to press that little bit harder, hitting at a time when you are figuring out who you are, as you go through significant physical and mental development.

It breaks my heart to see young people struggle with such deep identity crisis. With large sections of the media constantly telling you what to wear, what to like, how to fit in, and ultimately who to be, it can be almost impossible to accept yourself for who you are if you don't naturally fit the 'model' (of which I'm pretty sure only about 3 people in the world actually do). If you search for your identity anywhere other than in your Creator, you will come unstuck. When we act exclusively on the impulses of our own hearts, or through the influences of others, we take another step away from the person that God created us to be. Only He knows and loves you perfectly; only He knows the reason for which you were created; and only He, through His death and resurrection, has made it possible for you to live out those purposes!

Spiritual discipline is not just about giving things up. God wants to be in relationship with you, to help and guide you, to reveal his purposes for your life. Spiritual discipline helps us in our relationship with God when we commit to praying, studying His Word, worshipping, meditating, fasting, and giving. Through these disciplines we begin to find our identity in Christ more fully, and it is our obedience to God that brings about the transformation that we want God to effect in our lives. Do you see how this ties in with the fruit of faithfulness? Why not take another look and at that chapter and see how these areas overlap. Are you starting to see how these aspects of the fruit of the Spirit cannot be separated? They all work together as a whole!

Let me take this opportunity to say that God is NOT a spoil-sport or party-pooper! God wants us to enjoy life, and enjoy it to the full! Jesus tells us, in John 10:10, that He has come to give us "a rich and satisfying life". Do you believe Him, or do you think He is a party judge who has given you the sentence of life without the possibility of fun parole?

Having made us, God knows how we work best. He knows what is good for us, and, like any parent, must set the guides for their child's welfare. If God tells you getting drunk is a bad idea, it is the same principle as the Apple Corporation telling you your iPhone will stop working if you throw it in a fire. They made it, they know it. It's not rocket science, really. Being responsible for our own behaviour, however, is part of the freedom that we have in life. It is, of course, one of the easiest things to abuse (stop blaming your brother for everything!).

There's a very good reason self-control is an aspect of the fruit of the Spirit. God is asking us to think carefully about the things in life that do not glorify him and especially those things which lead us into sin. Jesus even goes so far as to say, in Matthew 5:30,

"...if your right hand causes you to sin, cut it off and throw it away."

Now, before you start reaching for the hacksaw, realise that Jesus is broadly calling us to identify the areas that cause us problems and to cut ourselves off from them. Going back to the alcohol example, if you know that drinking is going to lead to temptations and even cause you to sin, isn't it better to remove the problem completely than to risk falling into the trap of sin which draws you away from God?

Why not think of your own life, and the areas where maybe you need to be more disciplined? Challenge yourself to think about

REMIX:

Richard Foster wrote the classic Christian book 'Celebration of Discipline' in 1978. As relevant today as when it was first published, it looks at the importance of prayer, fasting, meditation and study for living a truly deep Christian life.

your actions and what they say about you. And, more importantly, if you have accepted God into your life, what they say about Him. Honour God with your actions and He will honour you. It is one of the greatest promises in the Bible. [*See deeper reading*.] Consider what you can do to grow in your relationship with, and understanding of, your Creator God through the disciplines of prayer, study, worship and so forth. Find your identity in Jesus and allow Him to reveal the fullness of life to you, so that you can share it with the world around you. The benefits will begin today, and last for eternity!

I'm living in the reality that one day I will be at the best party I will ever go to, and it will never end. Who will be the life and soul of *that* party?

Summary

- *Pursue self-discipline so that you may avoid unnecessary temptation and draw closer to God.*

- *Give over to God the areas of your life that you struggle to have discipline in and ask him to help transform your life.*

- *Honour God and he will honour you.*

Questions

1. What do you think of when you hear the word discipline?

2. Where do you find your identity?

3. What areas of your life need to be more disciplined for the benefit of your relationship with God?

4. What could you give up/take up to honour God?

Challenge

Agree with a friend to both give something up for a period of time. Why not be more ambitious than the typical 'Lent' period and try to do something for a whole year? If it is a television show, or something time consuming, use the time to read your Bible, or meet with your friend to talk about God and pray together. I guarantee that the dual discipline of both giving something up and committing to God time will deepen your relationship with him.

Prayer

Father God, help me to have more self-control in my life. I want to know you more and commit to spending more time with you every day. I ask forgiveness for the times when I sin, and I give over to you the areas of my life that I struggle to have discipline in. I pray that you will help me live in a way that honours you and encourages others. Amen.

CHASING AFTER:

PURITY

Shell Perris

I believe wholeheartedly that this generation should do everything in their power to live with purpose and intention and chase after holiness and purity. This is my prayer... pray it if you dare!

Father God,

Raise up a generation of young people who are completely and utterly sold out for you. Reveal to them the depths of your love and the magnitude of your character. Give them the ability to see you for who you really are, through every situation they may face in life. Give them the determination to follow you wherever you lead them, whatever the cost. Teach them how to die to themselves so that you can truly rise up within them. Give them the strength to live with purpose and walk with intention as they fulfil the plans that you have especially set out for them. Enable each one of them to display self-control as they strive to follow your examples of holiness and purity. Give them the courage to say 'No', even if it makes them unpopular. May this generation be an example to the world as they lay down their own agendas and abandon themselves to your will.

In the name of Jesus Christ,

Amen.

10.
the pursuit of...
GOD

Key Verses:

Philippians 1:6

And I am certain that God, who began the good work within you, will continue his work until it is finally finished on the day when Christ Jesus Returns.

Philippians 2:12

Dear friends, you always followed my instructions when I was with you. And now that I am away, it is even more important. Work hard to show the results of your salvation, obeying God with deep reverence and fear.

The Pursuit

So here we are. This is what it all comes down to, the climax of the book. If this was a Hollywood film, you might be anticipating a huge action-set piece right about now or a brain-bending twist in the tail of the story. Fans of romance novels would be holding their breath to see if true love takes its course; comic book readers would be excitedly anticipating just how the hero is going to save the day this time. Have I built it up enough yet? Good, because here it comes. Everything you have read up to here is pointless.

For those of you who have just performed a comedy double-take, you did read that correctly. Everything you have read this far is pointless, *if* you don't pay very close attention to this final chapter (okay, I know that was a bit sneaky. It was my attempt at the Hollywood twist!).

Joking aside, there is some truth to the statement above. This is the part of the book where we pull the previous nine pursuits together and focus them into one ultimate pursuit: the pursuit of God! You see without God none of what has come before has any meaning or any truth. God is the beginning to all of this, the starting point, and let's not forget that he is the end too. It all starts and ends with God. Now this is massively important so pay attention at the back (and stop doodling!). The challenge in this book is *not* 'pursue all the things in chapters one to nine and you will find God'. The challenge, without question, is to pursue God first, foremost, and at all costs and *then* these other things will follow.

Back in the days when I was a full-time schools worker my favourite lesson to lead was one about the existence of God. I would use various illustrations to explain why I, as a Christian, believed there was a God. But it was always the part of the lesson where I would explain the complexities and wonder of the human body that would amaze the kids the most and get them thinking about the potential for a creator God.

Recently, I've had the great pleasure of going into many schools and universities with my friend Chip Kendall (who, if you are reading this book from beginning to end, you will have already encountered in the first *Chasing After* section), and various professional scientists, to look at the whole area of science and faith. Are they compatible? Has science killed God? What are we to think of evolution and the big bang? That kind of stuff. I wasn't too hot at science when I was at school, but I've loved spending time with these different scientists, learning new

things from their respective fields of expertise.
The biologists, in particular, have opened my
eyes even wider to the complexity and wonder of
the human body, and this has only strengthened
my belief in some of the things I used to talk
about when I first went into schools more than
ten years ago.

I won't reel off all the facts here but, rest
assured, the human body is a very, very clever
creation. Every part and every organ has its job
(some of them can even multitask!) that will
keep us alive and functioning. Our whole body is
in co-operation with itself. If at any point one
part starts to do something it shouldn't or not do
its job properly we can be in trouble! We need all
the complicated aspects of our bodies to co-
operate with themselves for us to live!

I have found out the hard way in life that it's
almost as important for your brain and your
mouth to co-operate with each other!

A perfect example happened recently while I
was in a hotel bar waiting for service. I noticed
an elderly lady on crutches and in a neck brace
standing alone and looking decidedly down in the
dumps. Being the cheery chap I am, I decided to
spark up a conversation in a genuine attempt to
be pleasant. I opened my mouth with the words,
"Have you been in the wars, my love?", thinking

God

that she would have an opportunity to tell me about her recent fall to which I could respond with an appropriate amount of compassion and concern. Instead she replied, absolutely stone faced, "No. I have spinal arthritis."

I wasn't expecting that to be honest. Twisted ankle, sore back or dodgy hip would have all been acceptable responses but I, for some reason, was not expecting such a grim diagnosis. This unexpected turn of events threw my brain a sudden curveball and, as my mouth struggles to listen to my brain at the best of times, co-operation between the two ceased. All I could force out of my mouth in reply was the frankly hideous question, "Oh...does that get better in the sunshine?"

I know, I know, I literally have no idea what I was thinking. She looked at me as if I was mentally disturbed and replied, with a suitable amount of venom, "It never gets better!".

Deeper Reading:

2 Pet 1:3-9

Heb 13:20-21

Col 2:6-10

Jam 2:14-17

2 Thes 2:13-17

1 Tim 6:12

The Pursuit

There ended the conversation.

When co-operation doesn't happen, the world has witnessed, and been subject to, much more serious consequences than an ill-judged conversation. Wars have started, famines have plagued nations and communities have been torn apart through intolerance, to give just a few examples. Yet co-operation between people sees peace prevail, resources distributed in a way that the hungry can be fed and differences combated so that communities are united. A co-operative world is not a divided world.

Have you ever been in a team situation where there was little or no willingness to co-operate with each other? It never works! Think of the greatest sports teams of all time or the best bands or dance and theatre groups. Do you think that they would have had the success and acclaim they are known for if every member was not prepared to co-operate with each other? Of course not! You will often hear groups that co-operate well with each other referred to as 'well-oiled machines', every part doing its job for the success of the whole. When one individual, or one person's agenda, becomes more important than another, unwilling to compromise or make sacrifice, we lose our ability to co-operate and the consequences can be devastating. This is nowhere more true than in our relationship with God, which has to be, you guessed it, co-operative.

God wants to work in your life, in fact he has begun this work in you already! Check out the first of our key verses in Philippians 1:6,

"And I am certain that God, who began the good work within you, will continue his work until it is finally finished on the day when Christ Jesus returns."

What a fantastic promise! God is committed to seeing your life transformed (and your soul saved!) because of who he is. However, the danger is that with that truth in mind we become passive followers of Jesus. We sit and wait for God to do his work in us. If that is the message you take away from this book then you have missed the whole point (and like I said at the top, everything that has come before in this book is made pointless!). There are things that we can, and must, do for ourselves that God will not do for us! There is a huge responsibility on our shoulders laid out in the second of our key verses, which also comes from Philippians, a little later on, in chapter 2:12,

The Pursuit

"Dear friends, you always followed my instructions when I was with you. And now that I am away, it is even more important. Work hard to show the results of your salvation, obeying God with deep reverence and fear."

Paul is very clear in these verses about the two-sided nature of the work involved in our relationship with God. We are called to co-operate with God in a way that allows him to do his work in our lives whilst doing all we can to reveal the transformation of our lives to the world.

It comes down to your character. Are you prepared to walk and

REMIX:

It seems like from the moment we were created people have had questions for and about God. C.S Lewis' 'Mere Christianity' (1952) was a life-changing book for me, dealing with some of the big questions of faith. Timothy Keller's 'The Reason For God' (2007) is a modern take on some of the same themes. See what inspiration you can take from these great thinkers, and consider your responses to the questions your friends and family have about God.

live in a way that both deepens your own knowledge of God and also reveals more of him to the world? That is what God wants from you, and that is what the world needs from you. Don't get caught up just in the things that God does but instead invest your life in who he *is*. It is about truly knowing God and knowing him will lead to the fruit of the Spirit in your life. That is why he must be (and is!) the beginning. The knowledge of him will transform your life inside-out and that transformation, worked out in your life, can in turn transform the world! But don't passively sit around and wait for him to change you before you follow the call. Get stuck in now! We are all works in progress!

Equally, for those of you who are a little over-confident, do not think you can achieve it in your own strength. Pride, as they say (actually, as the Bible says!), does often come before a fall, and, as soon as you believe you can do a little bit in your own strength, you will keep giving yourself more and more credit until one day you will believe you have no need of God's strength. One of the most significant tricks Satan works in people's lives is convincing them that they can do it themselves. He is all too aware that we are prone to a little pride as human beings, and the moment you rely on your own strength rather than God's is the moment that you buy into the lie that you can do it on your own, without Him. If that were true, then Jesus wouldn't have needed to die on the cross. God would never have sent Him. Instead, God knows that we need Him, and He graciously gives us a way to have life, through the greatest act of love the world has ever seen.

If I'm asked to give a basic gospel presentation, I usually come at it from the perspective of God being the King of the universe. He is the only one who has the power and authority to rule the universe, as He created and sustains it. Without Him, the universe could neither continue, nor exist in the first place. Each of us must decide if we want Him to be the King of our life, or if *we* want to be the King (or Queen) of our own life. Here is the amazing thing: God will not force His kingship on you; He will let *you* decide. When we say 'yes' to God being our King, it means we hand over the rule of our life to Him completely. We commit to faithfulness and obedience in all things. As equally amazing as it is that He would even give us this freedom to choose, is the gift that He gives us when we accept Him as King - Himself. His Holy Spirit moves into your life and takes up residence there, ready to guide, empower, sustain and speak to you. The more you co-operate with God as He lives in your life, fully relying on His strength but being obedient in the things He calls you to, the more you will see the fruit we have looked at in this book be present in, and flow out of, your life.

God wants to impact your life in incredible ways, if you are willing to co-operate and let Him work in you! The challenge is for us to get to work now, and then let him empower us far beyond what we are capable of.

That is co-operation with God.

That will lead to the fruit of the Spirit impacting all that you are.

That will transform your life.

That will transform the world.

That will bring God glory.

That is our life's pursuit.

Summary

- *Everything starts and ends with God.*

- *God has begun a work in you. Will you work with him to see it completed?*

- *Our life's pursuit is to truly know, co-operate with, and be changed by God, so that he will be glorified, and the world will be transformed.*

Questions

1. Who is God?

2. What does it mean to co-operate with Him?

3. What is the pursuit of your life?

4. How can you apply what you have read in this book into your life?

Challenge

Produce your own 'Chasing After' article - like the ones in this book - about what you think your generation should be pursuing. If writing is not your thing, why not make a short film, write a song, interview your friends on your smartphone... Whatever your preferred method, use it to communicate your heart for your own generations pursuit. I'd love to see what you come up with so post them on our Facebook page: fb.com/generationnowuk

or email me your creations direct at: ben@generation-now.co.uk

Prayer

Father God, Lord Jesus Christ, Holy Spirit. It is my hearts desire to know you more deeply, more truly, and more completely. May all that I do, and all that I am, lead me to that greater knowledge of you, so that I will be transformed for your glory. May the pursuit of my life be you. May the fruit of your Spirit be present in my heart. And, may the sacrifice of your son be my foundation. Amen.

CHASING AFTER:

SACRIFICE

Chris Jack

Sacrifice. That was the one-word title of a little book on the Christian life that I read many years ago, and that impacted me very deeply. I know it's a bit of an old-fashioned word and does not have a trendy, contemporary ring to it, but then I guess I'm an old-fashioned guy. Then again, part of our popular culture or not, sacrifice is very much a reality in our world today. Just think of the soldiers in Iran, or Afghanistan, who in your lifetime have made the ultimate sacrifice in carrying out their duty, striving to make the world a better, safer place for others.

The Pursuit

And sacrifice is very much a biblical reality. Paul, in Romans 12:1, calls believers to "present your bodies as living sacrifices . . ." Wow. That's strong stuff. What he is saying is that as Christians we are like sacrifices that have been killed and laid on an altar—except that we are still alive ('living sacrifices')! But now our life has been offered as a sacrifice to God, and it is his not ours. What that means in practice is that we don't live selfishly, for ourselves, doing just what pleases us and makes us 'happy,' or whatever. Instead, we put him first, even when it costs us, even when it hurts. That has big implications for how we live our lives, not least in our relationships with others (family, friends etc.). And that will always cost us. Putting God first, and putting others before ourselves, will call on us at times to make real sacrifices.

Jesus said, "Greater love has no one than this, that he lay down his life for his friends." (John 15:13). That's what he did. Most of us will not be called on to make that ultimate sacrifice, but what will we lay down, or give up (comforts, gadgets, luxuries, time, energy, rights, preferences, conveniences, having our own way—the list is endless) for God and for others? We live in a very me-oriented, me-centred society that emphasises pampering ourselves and pandering to every little whim and fancy that we have: spoiling ourselves, "because you're worth it." Jesus calls us, as his followers, to live in a different way: denying ourselves (Matthew 16:24), and living sacrificially. The pursuit of sacrifice, not for its own sake or for show, but as a deliberate, thoughtful life-response to Jesus is my call (actually, it's *his* call!) to this generation.

11.
the pursuit of...
SILENCE

Key Verses: Mark 1:35-37

Before daybreak the next morning, Jesus got up and went out to an isolated place to pray. Later Simon and the others went out to find him. When they found him, they said, " Everyone is looking for you."

The Pursuit

I like to talk; a lot. Seriously, ask anyone who knows me and they'll tell you, I'm a talker. Now, it's not that I don't like to listen as well. If the conversation is flowing, I'm all ears. I just like to keep things moving; I'm not exactly known for my silences.

It's not just in conversation, either. I'm the kind of person that needs to have noise around me all the time. If I'm walking to the shops, the iPod goes in the ears. If I'm alone in the house, the TV goes on for background noise. Lying in bed trying to fall asleep, I'll stick a podcast on and let the voices send me to my dreams. I've often wondered why it is that I like sound so much. After all, I'm a DJ, so a big part of my life involves using sounds to create a great experience for people. I guess that maybe I'm just more comfortable when there is noise than when there isn't.

I travel around to all sorts of events during the year. I've experienced just about every kind of youth service, celebration, and festival going. One thing I've often noticed is a common trend when it comes to the 'response time', which usually takes place as the speaker is drawing the theme of the event to a close with some kind of call to commitment, or declaration. More often than not, as the speaker moves from their 'talk'

Deeper Reading:

2 Pet 1:3-9

Eccl 3:7

1 Kings 19:11-13

Job 2:11-13

Psa 46:10

Matt 14:23

into the 'response', music will begin to play. It might be the keyboard player of the worship band who, using ninja-like skills, has crept back onto the stage to provide the ambient soundtrack to the moment at hand. Other times I've seen the whole band begin to play, a DJ spinning some background tunes, video clips with meditative images and sound. Whatever the source, the idea is the same - creating an atmosphere that is helpful for those who are thinking about responding to the message.

I remember being at one event when a friend of mine was playing keys in the worship band. It was agreed beforehand that during the response time he would come on stage and start playing some background music. After his initial suggestions of a few Elton John covers were shot down (joke, but I'd be all for it), everything was set for the response. Sure enough, after an impassioned preach, the speaker began to call people to respond to the message and my friend began to play his keys (keyboard that is - I have yet to see a worship response bashed out on a couple of car keys).

The more he played, the more he could feel the atmosphere of the room. He closed his eyes and began to personally worship, playing beautiful melodies that would surely lead people into the presence of God. The only problem was, whilst he could hear his keyboard perfectly in his in-ear monitors, nothing was coming out of the speakers to the crowd. The entire response was done in silence, whilst, on stage in front of everyone, under the impression all could hear as he could, my friend was going for it Stevie Wonder style. Awkward.

Silence often is awkward. The fear of a first date is usually that of sitting in silence over coffee or dinner, realising you have absolutely nothing to talk about. The problem is, in our quest to eradicate the awkwardness of silence, have we lost the ability to really listen to God, to create space where he can be heard?

There is a double challenge here, because for us to find space for the silence we will have to do something else that many of us struggle with - get some alone time.

Silence

Our world is designed now to be primarily a social place. Even when we can't physically meet face to face, the internet has provided us with numerous other opportunities to socialise. Our church communities are based around spending time together, at youth groups, home groups, services, special social events and so on. This is largely good stuff; spending time with each other, building relationships and investing in each other's lives is a central theme of the gospel. I do wonder, however, if we are heading for a culture, both inside and outside of the church, that becomes so obsessed with the need to be social that it forgets the importance of solitude. You see, sometimes, God just wants to spend time with you, and you alone.

It will probably come as no surprise to hear that one of the biggest fears people have is the fear of being alone. We all want to have friends, don't we? And, going beyond that, most people hope eventually to meet that special someone who may end up becoming the future Mr or Mrs you. This deeper romantic relationship, for many people, becomes the ultimate pursuit of their life, and, for those who don't find it immediately, or ever, it can become a source of great sadness.

In some churches, marriage is seen as the ideal for *everyone*, and some churches I go to seem more like dating agencies than anything else! Despite the fact that I believe we should explore and embrace singleness more openly in the church (although that's a topic for another book entirely), relationships - romantic or otherwise - are one of the most wonderful (and at times infuriating!) things about living this life. There's a reason for this.

We were created for fellowship and relationship with our God and each other. We were never meant to be alone! Where we sometimes get it wrong, though, is in trying to satisfy our need for relationship primarily through other people. God wants us to have great human relationships and friendships, but He wants to be the most important relationship in our life. He wants to be the centre of all that we are; and, in so being, the centre of all our relationships.

Good relationships sometimes need to be a little bit selfish. Spending time exclusively alone with a friend, to have and share in each other's full attention for a time, can be essential in strengthening and deepening your connection. It is the same with our relationship with God. There are times when He wants your complete, undivided attention. He wants to speak clearly to you, to bless you, to encourage you, to convict you, to refresh you, to challenge you, to heal you. In the hustle and bustle of this world and our busy social schedules, often the most effective and faithful way for us to honour our relationship with God is to take ourselves away from everything and everyone else, to do away with the noise, and to listen to our God.

The Bible gives us loads of examples of people taking the time to get space and solitude with God; not least Jesus. Jesus knew how important it was to hear from the Father: for encouragement,

REMIX:

Certain orders of monks and nuns live out almost completely silent lives. This is called monastic silence, and even has its own types of sign language! What can you find out about this kind of monastic living and why do you think these people commit themselves to such a discipline?

refreshment, and instruction. Forty days in the desert, removing himself from the crowds (and the disciples) at Capernaum, and his time in the garden of Gethsemene before his arrest, are all revelations to us of a Jesus who values prayer and solitude with his Father. There is no question

that during these so called 'wilderness'
experiences Jesus would have spent time in
silence, waiting on his Father's voice. If Jesus,
fully human, but also who was and is fully God,
needed to do such a thing, how much more must
we!

Creating space for God doesn't have to be
an awkward experience; especially when we are
on our own. Those first date silences will be
painful, but zoom forward forty years of marriage
and the silences that come will be much more
comfortably and naturally played out. The more
you wait silently on God, the more comfortable
you will become.

But, I would go further than just suggesting
it as a personal activity and encourage it when
we are gathered together in our churches and at
our events, too. The temptation can be to create
an environment where God can move through an
emotive musical soundtrack. Watch any thrilling
Hollywood movie without the soundtrack and it
will lose some of its impact. The music is
designed to increase the power of the scene on
the viewer. We use a similar technique in our
gatherings which has a power that can be helpful
in stirring our hearts, but can also hinder when it
promotes emotional response over a true focus
on what God is saying to his people.

Silence

We do a great job of filling our lives, church gatherings, camps and festivals with noise. God has given us a beautiful tool in music, through which, although not exclusively, we can worship, meditate and focus on him. This is not a call to do away with all of this. However, we have a rich biblical heritage of people who give themselves the space and silence they need to hear from, and then be obedient to, their Father God. Isn't it time we learned from their example?

My challenge to myself is to spend time every day, silently, alone with God. Through prayer and study of His Word I want to commit to giving him the space to speak to me so that I might know him better. It may turn out to be the most comfortable and natural thing I ever do.

However, I'm prepared for it to be awkward. I'm prepared for it to be uncomfortable. And I'm prepared for it to be all about him. Are you?

Summary

- *God wants to speak to you today!*

- *We need to create space in our busy lives to stop, retreat to a silent place and listen to God.*

- *We can push past our own awkwardness until we find it completely natural to spend time alone with our Father God.*

Questions

1. *Do you find it easy or difficult to spend time silently alone with God?*

2. *What does it mean to 'listen' to God?*

3. *Why are solitude and silence important in our relationship with God?*

4. *What can we learn from how Jesus approached his relationship with his father?*

Challenge

Put a date in your diary for sometime in the next month where you will take yourself away into the wilderness for an entire morning or afternoon (or a whole day if you are really up for the challenge!). Find a safe but secluded location where you will not be disturbed and that is naturally quiet. Take a bible, a notepad and a pen with you. Use the time to simply listen to God, and write down what you hear. Make this a regular retreat and see how it shapes your relationship with God over the coming months.

Prayer

Father God, I am sorry that I do not create the silence and space in my life that I need to hear from you clearly. I commit to listening for your voice as often as I can, and I pray that you will speak to me so that I may know you more. May the silent times I spend with you be loudly revealed in my life to the world around me. For your glory. Amen.

CHASING AFTER:

THE TRINITY

Jamie Hill

When I proposed to my wife Naomi, I didn't just want to do something 'normal'. This woman was, hopefully, going to agree to spend the rest of her life with me. She knew so many of my faults, weaknesses, and sins, and had the choice then to take all of that on, or not. As I thought about how to ask her, I thought about her – about who she is and what she likes. Without that I would have had no idea how to ask in a way that really showed how much I cared. As the string quartet played her favourite music, on the side of the lake by the bridge covered with candles all the way to the bonfire on the island, and as she started to cry as she saw all that I had done, and how I had made it all about her, I knew that I had done my best. The outcome was then down to her, but she knew that I loved her, and knew her. I hope!

Who she was changed everything. Who she was decided every part of that night. The things she liked, I wanted to make happen. I wanted it to be the perfect night for her.

Who God is changes everything. I am really concerned that many of us don't really know who our God is. If we don't know who He is, we won't understand Him. We will struggle to understand what He likes and how justice, love and mercy can dwell perfectly together. If we don't know who He is, then we can end up with a view of Him being one thing in the Old Testament and then another in the New Testament, rather than get a picture of the fullness of who this amazing God is.

The key to knowing who our God really is lies in this so often misunderstood and mis-taught doctrine of the Trinity. Whilst 'Trinity' doesn't exist as a term in the Bible, it isn't a last minute idea to try and make sense of God. It is the thing that defines the God of the scriptures and makes Him so different to Allah or any other single-person God. Very well-intentioned people teach different things in trying to help us

understand the Trinity and who our God is, my
favourite being Aquafresh toothpaste: three
strands doing different things in one toothpaste.
But there are lots of others, such as God is like
water expressed in three states: liquid, gas
(steam) and solid (ice). The problem with so
many of these illustrations is that they paint an
unclear and untrue picture of God. For instance,
the water illustration infers that God is one being
who chooses to show himself in different modes
or states, not three constant parts of one God.
This doesn't really work with key stories in the
Bible that infer the triune nature of God, such as
the baptism of Jesus.

So what is the Trinity? The Trinity is Father,
Son and Spirit. All God. All eternal. They have
always been Father, Son and Spirit together, in an
intimate relationship of love. This is not love as
we may know it. It's bigger; it's purer; it's ever
flowing from the Father, Son and Spirit to each
other. How can we know this? John 17:24 tells us
that Jesus was loved by the Father before the
creation of the world. So what we realise about
the Father here is that before creation or
anything else, he was what? A Father. A loving,
besotted Father.

I have recently become a Dad and I am
head-over-heels in love with my little girl; she

rocks my world and I would do anything for her. This is who God the Father is and has been from the beginning of time. Jesus has always been there, and been His Son. The Father has always been a Father, and the Son has always been a Son. This is an amazing revelation and shifts everything. If God was just a single person, how could he be loving unless he created something to love? So he would need his creation. Our God doesn't need us, but because His love is constantly flowing out from Father, to Son, to Spirit, to Father, He creates to let this infectious love spread out and bring US into that loving relationship. WOW! This is the gospel. Not just that Jesus has paid the price for us, but that we are invited into this relationship because through Jesus we are now children of God. This means the loving Father that has always been an amazing Daddy, is now our Daddy! This is incredible. Do you see how our understanding of our God changes everything?

Jesus is the very

"… radiance of God's glory and the exact representation of his being, sustaining all things by his powerful word. After he had provided purification for sins, he sat down at the right hand of the Majesty in heaven." (Hebrews 1:3)

Chasing After: The Trinity

So Jesus is the full representation of the Father. It is the Father's full ever-flowing love that sends the Son, who shows us the fullness of this love, and welcomes us and the whole of creation to become little love-receivers and love-givers to the world.

The Holy Spirit makes the love of the Father known to the Son and to us (2 Corinthians 1:21-22).

The key to this is that what defines the Father, Son and Spirit is not necessarily what they do but the relationship that they have together. It is that relationship that defines our God and helps us understand what it means to love and follow Him.

Martin Luther, one of the key leaders of the shift in the church called the Reformation, defined sin as man curved in on himself. He taught that all sin in the Bible, and in life, can be boiled down to us as humans turning away from God and turning in on ourselves, becoming driven by our own desires and away from God's best for us. This is the complete opposite to what our outward-looking, outward-loving trinity God is all about. So how do we stop curving in on ourselves?

Mike Reeves in his excellent book *The Good God* says:

191

The Pursuit

"Naturally I am bent in on myself and I take an hellish delight in my own supposed independence. But if I am to be anything like the outgoing and outward-looking Father, Son and Spirit, the Spirit must take my eyes off myself (which he does by winning me to Christ)."

This is what our God is about. The full gospel is that you and I are called into an eternal relationship of constant, outflowing love. We are not just called to one part of this trinity; each part draws us to relationship with each of the other parts. Love from before time is there for us from the Father, through the Son in the power of the Holy Spirit. This is our God.

So which God will you have? Will you settle for a lesser God, or pursue this amazing Trinity that eternally loves out, loves us and calls us to do the same?

The End Of
The Beginning

This book is only the beginning! This is where you now have to take the challenge beyond the pages of this book and into your life. God wants to use you to transform this world and he wants to start today.

As I said in the introduction to this book, the purpose here is not to teach you how to pick and choose which fruit you want in your life. You can't have a bit of kindness and drop of goodness and forget about the rest! It doesn't work like that. When thinking about the fruit of the spirit, the key is to remember there is no 's' on the end of the word fruit. No plural. One spiritual fruit with nine aspects (or virtues). This book is about the reality that when we fully pursue God, all those amazing aspects of the fruit of the spirit can be, and should be, present in our lives. One will flow from another. Pursue God first with all you have and see if you begin to recognise his character in you.

If *The Pursuit* has impacted you, why not share it with someone else? Maybe you could start a Bible study using the chapters of this book (including the deeper reading and questions and challenges) as a basis for your discussions. However you use, and respond to, this book I would love to hear from you via email:

ben@generation-now.co.uk

One thing I should definitely say before we wrap things up is that there is nothing in this book that is not more amazingly and truthfully revealed in the Bible. I literally cannot encourage you enough to spend time every day reading about the God you are living for. He has given us the perfect resource to grow in our knowledge of him. If you haven't already looked up all the deeper reading sections then don't even think about finishing with this book until you do! And, if you are really keen (and I hope you are!) then get hold of as many of the books recommended in the library card sections as you can and take your reading and study to the next level!

Many of the contributors in *The Pursuit* are involved with ministries and organisations that may be able to help train, encourage or equip you as you move forward. Take some time to explore the contributors page at the back of the book and visit their respective websites; I'm confident you will find something to help you as you continue on your journey.

Well that's it, the end of the beginning. Where you go from here is down to you but this prayer of commitment might be a good way to start the next unwritten chapter,

Mighty Father God,

I commit to living out an authentic lifestyle that reveals more of you to my family, my friends or even a stranger who notices something different in the way that I live. I pray that this is just the beginning of my pursuit of you. Thank you that I can know you more because of what Jesus has done. May the fruit of your spirit be full in my life so that others may encounter you and begin their own pursuit.

Amen.

Amen.

GENERATION NOW

Thank-you for purchasing this book. Every sale directly supports the ministry of Generation Now.

Generation Now is a Christian youth ministry that exists to engage young people and young adults in dialogue about issues of faith and life.

YOUR FAITH

Everyone makes a decision about their faith at some point, and wherever you choose to put your faith will have a huge impact on how you live your life. We believe that faith should not be a default decision for anyone, but should be thought through and evaluated.
From that basis, our work revolves around three key areas:

Evangelism - *Where do you put your faith?*
Discipleship - *How faithful are you to that faith?*
Church - *How do you share in your faith?*

In both listening and speaking to young people about these questions, we hope they will learn the skills they need to evaluate their faith effectively, and make decisions that they understand, commit to, and live for.

GOD'S STORY

Life is a story. Like all good stories it has a beginning, a middle and an end. It will involve highs and lows, twists and turns. Characters will come and go, changing and shaping the narrative as they do. The story may not always go the way you expect, or want it to, but one thing is for sure, the choices you make will have a huge impact on how it plays out.

But what if your story was actually part of a bigger story? What if the author of your story was trying to communicate with his creation? What if your story was really God's story? Generation Now is committed to helping young people and young adults explore their story, working through the good chapters, and the bad. Looking at the plot holes, talking through the unexpected twists and turns.

Generation Now is passionate about seeing young people connect with their author and creator, and through various projects and expressions, discover how their story is actually Gods story.

GENERATION NOW. YOUR FAITH, GOD'S STORY.

No matter how old or young, no matter what stage of the journey we are at, the one thing we all have in common is that we are in this life now. At Generation Now we believe the whole community has value and purpose. When you realise your story is part of God's story you can begin to discover what that purpose is, and through faith see your world transformed.

Will you be a part of his Generation Now?

Please visit www.generation-now.co.uk for resources and information about our projects. We would love to come and work with your group or event so we would love to hear from you.

ACKNOWLEDGEMENTS

To everyone who has played a part in getting this thing written a huge thanks! Give yourselves a pat on the back from me.

The story behind how this book came to be written is a good yarn in itself and I'd be happy to share it with anyone who fancies a coffee sometime, so long as you are paying. Ste Corner, Margaret Dimmock, Tabitha Rosebaum, Ken Mullis, Chip and Helen Kendall, Ruth Bancewicz, and Sharon Toop have all either directly been involved with this book or have influenced content. For that I am hugely grateful.

The beginnings of some of these thoughts can be traced back to another book I was collaborating on with two great friends, Simon Dayman and Andy Searle Barnes. We never finished that project chaps but hopefully anything I stole from that is well represented here!

Some of the chapters are adapted from thoughts and articles that I first wrote for the Cross Rhythms website (www.crossrhythms.co.uk) which is a fantastic resource for young people and a great place to go deeper on some of the thoughts raised in this book. Thanks in particular to Heather Bellamy for editing my work there so beautifully!

To all those who contributed something to the book and are named within its pages, thank you for your time and effort and adding a far greater depth than only my words could have had.

Andy Robinson, Alan Brand, Luke Taylor and the team and volunteers at Generation Now, thanks for your work, input and support.

To my family, your influence is all over this book and I am so thankful that you gave me the encouragement to be me in Jesus, which was the perfect foundation for writing this. What I have learned from my parents about grace, integrity, love and kindness would take a lifetime to get down on paper. Thank you Lord for the blessing they are to me and those who are fortunate enough to spend time with them. In particular thanks to Dad for giving so much of your valuable time to add wisdom, insight and a level of grammar that they just don't teach any more! Genuinely couldn't have finished this without your help, and for that reason I am finally able to forgive you for dragging me up mountains as a kid.

Thank you God for pursuing me first.

CONTRIBUTORS

Riley Armstrong travels performing music and comedy across North America. He is also the Creative Arts Director at Bayside Auburn Church in Auburn, California, where he lives with his wife Shannon and their son Zeffren.
www.rileyarmstrong.com

Amy Burns is part of the Vine Church in Stockton, often found hosting & speaking at services and co-ordinating the 'muffin ministry' - loving the local students by giving away home-made muffins! Amy has a fascination with words and loves to write all kinds of things, which is useful as she's currently working on her PhD thesis in English Literature and blogs for a variety of different sites including Generation Now. One day she'll write a book. Honest. But in the meantime she loves using words and love to share the heart of Jesus with whomever she comes across.

Ben Cooley and his wife Deb are the founders of Hope For Justice. They started Hope For Justice after hearing about the plight of trafficked people around the world and feeling compelled to help. Ben and Debbie are passionate about provoking the church to practical action and seeing those in slavery rescued. Their heart is to inspire a generation to rise up against the injustice of human trafficking and see God restore lives that have been broken. They speak regularly across the UK sharing the vision of Hope For Justice, and their work often takes them on overseas trips to link up with anti-slavery projects working on the frontline. For more information about the work of Hope for Justice visit www.hopeforjustice.org.uk

Andy Flannagan is the director of the Christian Socialist Movement based at Labour Party HQ and Parliament – www.thecsm.org.uk. They exist to be a prophetic voice to left-sided politics and the church, encouraging Christians to see politics as mission. A driving passion is to see a just re-wiring of the global economic system. Andy continues to perform, speak, lead worship and play a lot of cricket. His proudest moment as an Irishman was captaining England's Barmy Army during the last Ashes series. His new worship songs and resources are available for free from www.andyflan.com.

Contributers

Steve Gambill is the founder/director of Rocknations. Originally from the USA Steve became Youth pastor at Abundant Life Bradford in 1993, launched the Rocknations conference in 2001. Since then, Rocknations has become one of the fastest growing conferences of its kind, impacting thousands of young people who attend Rocknations. Find out more about Rocknations at www.rocknations.com

Sam Hargreaves co-leads engageworship.org with his wife Sara. He completed the LST degree in Theology, Music and Worship, and now teaches in the department two days per week. He also co-leads RESOUNDworship.org, the free worship song website, and has led musical and creative worship at events like Spring Harvest, New Wine North and the Baptist Assembly alternative stream. Their book 'How would Jesus lead worship' was published by BRF in 2009.

Jamie Hill is the Head of Mission Development for the message trust and lives in Manchester. He's married to Naomi and has a beautiful little girl called Talitha. Jamie has worked for many churches, YFC and the bible society and loves

opening the bible to young people and painting a
bigger picture of the gospel than we so often
settle for. Jamie has also toured with many bands
as well as recording his own material.
www.message.org.uk

Chris Jack is Lecturer in applied theology at the
London School of Theology, where his areas of
special interest are John's Gospel, Worship and
Discipleship. He is passionate about helping
people, young and old, get a better
understanding of their faith and a deeper
commitment to living it out. He is married to
Babs, and they have two grown children of which
Ben is one! For information on studying at LST
visit www.lst.ac.uk

Chip Kendall was born in the USA, raised in
Israel, and spent his teen years touring the world
with his musical family. After 10 years performing
and speaking with thebandwithnoname, Chip
Kendall has now gone solo. He continues to
broadcast regularly, as a youth presenter on both
Cross Rhythms and GodTV, and has co-written a
number of books with his wife Helen. Be it
through his music, books or speaking

engagements Chip is a passionate evangelist who is excited about connecting Heaven to Earth. www.chipkendall.com

Shell Perris is an evangelist, singer, songwriter, speaker and author. Her passion is to get people of all ages excited about God and to let the world know that He is head-over-heels in love with every single one of us. Her bubbly personality and powerful life-story challenge and inspire the hearts of many. She is married to Tim and lives in Warrington, Cheshire, UK. www.shellperris.com

Mike Taylor has been a Youth Pastor in local church ministry in the United States for almost 30 years. Throughout his ministry, he has used his spiritual gifts to preach and teach students. Now living in the North East of England, he is the pastor of the Vine church in Stockton-on-Tees and the director of Tees Valley Youth For Christ. Mike graduated from the University of Arkansas and loves watching his "Hogs" play any sport. He and his wife Kookie have four children Thad, Shelby, Hannah and Hayden. www.yfc.co.uk